CUE CARD

CUE CARD

THE PEOPLE'S CHAMPION

EDITED BY
**LEE MOTTERSHEAD AND
ANDREW PENNINGTON**

RACING POST

In memory of Bob Bishop. He had many memorable days racing but his highlight was Cue Card winning the King George.

First published in Great Britain in 2018 by
Racing Post Books
27 Kingfisher Court, Hambridge Road, Newbury, Berkshire, RG14 5SJ

10 9 8 7 6 5 4 3 2 1

A catalogue record for this book is available from the British Library.

ISBN 978-1-910497-81-4

Cover designed by Nathan Bines

Printed in the Czech Republic by Finidr

Every effort has been made to fulfil requirements with regard to copyright
material. The author and publisher will be glad to rectify any omissions at
the earliest opportunity.

www.racingpost.com/shop

Photographic acknowledgements
All the photos are copyright © Racing Post except the following:
Bill Selwyn: page 37
Caroline Norris: page 45
Cranhamphotos: pages 17, 43, 52, 112, 146
Getty Images: pages 51, 81, 89, 93, 101, 110, 111, 119, 145, 149,
154–155, 160, 161
Grossick Racing: pages 22–23, 31, 59, 61, 70, 87, 102, 103, 133, 151
Martin Lynch: pages 91, 97, 98

All proceeds due to Mrs Bishop from sales of this book will be donated
to horse welfare charities.

CONTENTS

INTRODUCTION
Lee Mottershead

This is the story of a horse.

It is far from a short story, being of rather epic proportions in length and content, although to break it up there are intermissions, most of which were conducted on long, lush summer grass. The fact you are starting it suggests you know what happened, how it began and how it finished, but like all the best tales, it loses nothing when repeated.

The story's hero became, by common consent, the sport's most popular racehorse. Such standing is not easily achieved. Admiration can be gained quickly. Affection is much harder to forge. Cue Card secured both and for good reason.

To suggest this is a rags-to-riches journey would be overly romantic, not least because none of the people connected to the horse started the marathon on the bottom rung of racing's ladder. Equally, however, Cue Card was sent off a 40-1 outsider for the 2010 Champion Bumper because, although tremendously impressive on his first racecourse outing, he was trained by Colin Tizzard and neither punters, bookmakers nor pundits associated Colin Tizzard with Grade 1 success at the Cheltenham Festival.

Back then Tizzard was best known as someone who milked cows not championship races. Over the course of Cue Card's career that changed. Tizzard is now one of British jump racing's most dominant forces, blessed with expensive horses owned by inordinately wealthy clients. That development has come thanks to his talent as a trainer but the man himself readily admits the part played by Cue Card in his stable's rise was immense.

Tizzard is therefore a central character in this story, as is his son, Joe. Paddy Brennan makes plenty of appearances, and at times provides some of the best lines, while the colours of Jean Bishop,

Cue Card at the yearling sales

whose interest in racing was born through the involvement of late husband, Bob, became increasingly familiar on Britain's racecourses over the course of Cue Card's working life.

Ultimately, however, the true stars of horseracing are the horses and Cue Card was truly a star horse. Like a nationalised industry, he was publicly owned. The Bishops paid the bills. The rest of us shared in the pleasure and, occasionally, the pain.

There are highs and there are lows but throughout there is the horse we took to our hearts. Over the pages that follow you will be reminded why.

Joe Tizzard on Cue Card at Venn Farm

1
BUMPER START

FONTWELL
starspreads.com Standard Open
National Hunt Flat Race

2009-10   2010-11   2011-12   2012-13   2013-14
JAN FEB MAR APR | NOV DEC | JAN FEB MAR | APR | NOV DEC | JAN FEB MAR | APR | NOV DEC | JAN FEB | MAR | APR | NOV DEC | JAN FEB

Previous spread: Cue Card puts in
a flying leap during his victory in the
Grade 2 novice hurdle at Cheltenham
in November 2010

WHAT WAS ABOUT TO HAPPEN had never happened to them before. The Bishops and the Tizzards had for many years been deeply embedded in the sport of jump racing. For the Bishops, it was a passion and a hobby. To a significant extent the same had also been true of the Tizzards. The family business had been dairy farming. Racing was a hobby. It was to become rather more than that.

By the time Cue Card came along, Colin Tizzard had already trained good horses – but not many of them. He had initially taken out a point-to-point licence in 1995 to support amateur jockey son, Joe. Colin started training a few winners. Joe was even more prolific, so much so he became jump racing's champion conditional jockey and number-one rider to Paul Nicholls.

For Nicholls, Tizzard partnered a large number of high-class horses. For his father there were fewer, the best of them being the appropriately named Joe Lively, winner of the Grade 1 Feltham Novices' Chase on Boxing Day in 2007. The following season he captured two valuable prizes at Cheltenham, both times ridden by Joe. At that stage they were the most important winners Colin had ever sent out at jumping's home.

In November 2009, a smart animal called Mount Oscar won a £50,000 handicap chase on Newbury's Hennessy Gold Cup card. He was representing the Tizzard stable for only the second time, having made a successful debut for the yard at Fontwell one run earlier. By winning those two races, he got a new association off to a flying start.

Bob and Jean Bishop had been racing horses for two decades. Having been delighted with the job Joe Tizzard had done on their horses, including aboard Mount Oscar in his days with Richard Rowe, they decided to support his father. One of the horses they did that with was a King's Theatre gelding out of the mare Wicked Crack, acquired at the famous Tattersalls Ireland Derby Sale in June 2009.

The young animal, named Cue Card, had previously been bought in the same sales ring two years and four months earlier. On that occasion he was bought on behalf of owners Diana and Grahame Whateley for €75,000. After they eventually decided not to keep him, the Bishops made him theirs for just €52,000. Seven months later he was running in the couple's silks.

It would have been six months had the final two races at Exeter's card on Friday, December 4, 2009, not been abandoned due to poor visibility. The Bishops therefore had to wait until January 25, 2010, to see their new recruit, then a raw four-year-old, make his racecourse debut in the starspreads.com Standard Open National Hunt Flat Race, a contest staged over one mile, five and a half furlongs at Fontwell. Visibility this time was good. So was Cue Card.

This apparently came as no surprise to anyone. The Tizzards had told the Bishops the King's Theatre gelding was doing things at Venn Farm no other Venn Farm resident had done, certainly not the cows. He was the nap of the Racing Post's West Country correspondent Andrew King and duly stormed clear to win by six lengths, reporter Graham Dench noting the newcomer looked "every bit as good as the talk suggested he might be".

> **"**
> He is held in such regard that he will reportedly be given an entry in the Champion Bumper at the Cheltenham Festival"

RACING POST ANALYSIS: Cue Card cost connections €52,000 and immediately went some way to repaying them with a taking debut display. He made smooth headway when things began to get serious and responded strongly when asked to seal the race. He eventually came right away, looking suited by the soft ground and looks a very nice prospect. He is bred to stay further when going jumping, but is held in such regard that he will reportedly be given an entry in the Champion Bumper at the Cheltenham Festival.

Perhaps, given the reputation Cue Card carried with him to Fontwell, the surprise was he was allowed to be sent off as big as 6-1. This may well have reflected the fact that the racing public did not associate Colin Tizzard with potentially top-class horses, certainly not in the bumper division. Perhaps that is also why Cue Card was a 40-1 shot for his second race.

It was, however, no ordinary race. This was the Weatherbys Champion Bumper, the most important contest of its kind in the calendar. Among those in the field were subsequent multiple big-race

```
5.15    Weatherbys Champion Bumper
[OFF 5.15]   (Standard Open National Hunt Flat
        Race) Grade 1 Class 1   2m½f Old
For: 4,5,6-y-o 1st £34,206 2nd £12,834 3rd £6,426 4th £3,204 5th £1,608 6th £804
1    CUE CARD 4 10-12 ....................(121) Joe Tizzard
     b g by King's Theatre (IRE)–Wicked Crack (IRE) (King's Ride)
     (C L Tizzard) took keen hold, held up well in rear, scythed through
     field 5 out, tracked leader over 2f out and still cruising, led
     over 1f out, hung left briefly but romped clear   [op 33/1] 40/1
2   8 AL FEROF (FR) 5 11-5 ....................(128) R Walsh
     gr g by Dom Alco (FR)–Maralta (FR) (Altayan)
     (P F Nicholls) led, kept on well from 3f out, headed over 1f out,
     clear of rest but no chance with winner after   [bets of
     £25,000–£2,500 each-way, £8,000–£1,000(x2)}  [tchd 9/1] 8/1
3   8 FRAWLEY (IRE) 5 11-5 ....................(116)  B J Geraghty
     [16] b g by Catcher In The Rye (IRE)–Chauvire (Elmaamul (USA))
     (John E Kiely) held up in rear, not much room on inner over 5f out,
     progress from 4f out, tracked leaders 3f out, went 3rd over 1f out,
     outpaced   [bet of £80,000–£5,000 each-way]   [op 16/1] 14/1
```

winners Al Ferof and On His Own. There was, though, one better than both of them.

"He's as good a bumper horse as any we have had," Tizzard senior had said in the Racing Post preview on the morning of the race. "He is a really good horse," he added. "He has a turn of foot and the form of his Fontwell win has worked out. I wouldn't be surprised if he ran a really nice race."

As Tony Smurthwaite's Champion Bumper report made clear, he did exactly that.

Colin Tizzard did sound a warning, but few listened. Cue Card, the Dorset trainer said, was as good a bumper horse as he had trained. What if the once-raced winner was up against runners from the yards of champions, and others where the number of stablemates runs into three figures? It mattered not as Cue Card scored a sizzling victory at odds of 40-1, soaring to 61-1 on the Tote.

Toiling in second spot eight lengths down was the Paul Nicholls-trained Al Ferof, with the rest nowhere.

"I never thought he would do that," said Tizzard, meaning the brilliance of the triumph rather than its occurrence. "I don't understand why he was such a big price. If he was trained by Willie Mullins he would have been third or fourth favourite."

Ridden with supreme confidence by Joe Tizzard, the four-year-old son of King's Theatre was a first festival winner for his trainer and there could be some large cheques dangled in front of owners Jean and Bob Bishop, from near Eastbourne.

Tizzard senior added: "He pulled too hard and I thought, 'He'll stop in a minute.' It's lovely. We've not had many bumper horses, full stop."

Nicholls was pleased enough with Al Ferof, saying: "It was a great run and I should think they are two very good horses. Al Ferof will go hurdling in the autumn and is an exciting prospect."

What does that make the winner?

CHELTENHAM
Weatherbys Champion Bumper

RACING POST ANALYSIS: There was a shock winner in Cue Card, but it certainly looked no fluke as he won in impressive fashion reminiscent of Dunguib a year ago. Winner of a sub-2m bumper at Fontwell on his debut, form that has worked out well, he made eye-catching progress through the field and took over on the home turn before quickening clear, despite looking to be hanging. Still only four – he is the first winner from that age group since Dato Star in 1995 – he is out of a smart chaser and is a very bright jumping prospect.

It made him much more valuable than the €52,000 Bob and Jean Bishop had paid for him only nine months earlier.

Cue Card leaves Al Ferof and the rest of his Champion Bumper rivals trailing in his wake at the 2010 Cheltenham Festival

He is out of a smart chaser and is a very bright jumping prospect"

2014–15   2015–16   2016–17   2017–18

MAR | APR | NOV | DEC | JAN | FEB | MAR | APR | NOV | DEC | JAN | FEB | MAR | APR | NOV | DEC | JAN | FEB | MAR | APR | NOV | DEC | JAN | FEB | MAR | APR

That point was emphasised when Bob spoke to Rodney Masters for a piece that appeared in the Racing Post at the end of Cheltenham Festival week.

Jean and Bob Bishop are still on cloud nine following the success of Cue Card in the Weatherbys Champion Bumper.

When their 40-1 shot produced stunning acceleration to romp clear in the Champion Bumper, he was severing Ireland's six-year domination of the event. He was also the first four-year-old to win since Dato Star in 1995.

Bob Bishop says: "Joe told us on Wednesday night that when he went by Ruby Walsh [on runner-up Al Ferof] just over a furlong out, he heard two words from Ruby that indicated his surprise! The next morning we had a call from Colin. I asked him if he'd sold the horse yet, and he asked if I had. We've both had calls from interested people. But we're buyers, not sellers. We're going to enjoy him.

"We thoroughly enjoy our involvement with Colin and his family, who always make us feel so welcome when we go down to the stables.

"Having owned jumpers for so many years, we understand that there are inevitably more bad days than good ones, but our first win at the festival was exciting beyond words."

Over the days that followed, there was talk about whether Cue Card would see another festival in his first season. Mindful of the fact their young star could have years of top-level racing in front of him, the Bishops and Tizzards opted to play cautious and miss the major bumpers staged at Aintree and Punchestown.

Instead they waited and spent the summer dreaming about what Cue Card might achieve the following season. Indeed, such had been the impression he made when cruising into contention in the Champion Bumper, seemingly galloping at two to all his rivals' one, some even wondered if connections might be tempted to try their speedy star – whose sire had won the 1994 King George VI and Queen Elizabeth Stakes for Sir Henry Cecil – on the Flat.

> **"**
> We've both had calls from interested people. But we're buyers, not sellers. We're going to enjoy him"
>
> **BOB BISHOP**

Opposite: Joe Tizzard acknowledges the crowd as he returns on Cue Card to the Cheltenham winner's enclosure after the Champion Bumper

CHELTENHAM
Weatherbys Champion Bumper

He would not. There may have been the odd mention of a Flat foray, but all those associated with him were 100 per cent jumping people. Their horse would stay in jump racing. Moreover, the time had almost come when he would actually start to jump.

When Colin Tizzard staged his annual owners' day in September 2010, he observed: "The world is Cue Card's oyster." But where in the world would he reappear? On that early autumn afternoon, possible targets at Kempton, Exeter and Wincanton were suggested for an athlete already as short as 8-1 favourite for the Supreme Novices' Hurdle the following March.

The answer, after careful consideration, turned out to be Aintree.

Cue Card had long since been schooled over hurdles and had passed those early morning tests with flying colours, so hopes were high when he embarked on the second chapter of his career on Sunday, October 24, as 1-2 favourite in the two-and-a-half-mile European Breeders' Fund Bestway 'National Hunt' Novices' Hurdle.

"Ever since Cheltenham we have been waiting for this day," said Cue Card's trainer on the eve of the contest. As Tom O'Ryan reported, it had been well worth the wait.

Cue Card, whose demolition job in the Champion Bumper at the Cheltenham Festival in March marked him out as a potential star, underlined his limitless potential at Aintree when producing the most exhilarating performance of the jumps season so far.

Having made a mockery of his 40-1 odds when spreadeagling his rivals in the Weatherbys Champion Bumper at the festival, Cue Card hardly broke sweat in justifying a rather more cramped SP in yesterday's novice hurdle.

The Colin Tizzard-trained 1-2 favourite beat seven rivals by upwards of 13 lengths and, while his position at the head of the festival novice hurdles hardened, bookmakers were also inclined to quote him for the Stan James Champion Hurdle, for which he is a 33-1 shot with the sponsor.

The four-year-old, winner of both his bumper runs, was restrained by Joe Tizzard for much of his comeback outing

AINTREE
EBF Bestway 'National Hunt'
Novices' Hurdle

over 2m4f and, in a modestly run race, took a strong hold behind horses before being allowed to stride along once in line for home. He duly took the hint and burst clear of his rivals.

Tizzard senior, who trains Cue Card for Jean Bishop, was thrilled to see his stable star pass his first test with the minimum of fuss, saying: "He's done everything we thought he would do.

"From the first day we schooled him he's always been a great jumper – like a little pony – but he can be a bit keen, a bit excitable, when he comes to the races and we wanted to educate him and ride a race on him.

"It would have suited him if there had been a lot stronger pace – he wants that – but he's done it well in any case."

Looking to the future, he said: "We'll step him up in grade next time. The Cheltenham Open meeting is only three weeks away, but he's not taken anything out of himself, so we'll probably go there.

"I'll have to look and see what races he can run in. He could go over two and a half again, or he could come back to two miles, as he's got loads of pace. We'll learn more about him up to Christmas and then see where we're at with him."

Cue Card is a 6-1 chance for both the Supreme Novices' Hurdle and Neptune Investment Management Novices' Hurdle and is 3-1 with Blue Square to win any race at the festival.

"It's lovely and it's exciting," added Tizzard, "but there's also a lot of responsibility as well and you want to do everything right with him – horses like him don't come around very often."

RACING POST ANALYSIS: No Captain Chris, but this was perhaps still the most eagerly anticipated race of the weekend, with last season's deeply impressive Champion Bumper winner Cue Card, who had reportedly strengthened over the summer, making his debut over hurdles.

> **"**
> Horses like him don't come around very often"
> **COLIN TIZZARD**

2014-15   2015-16   2016-17   2017-18

MAR | APR | NOV | DEC | JAN | FEB | MAR | APR | NOV | DEC | JAN | FEB | MAR | APR | NOV | DEC | JAN | FEB | MAR | APR | NOV | DEC | JAN | FEB | MAR | APR

The form of the Cheltenham contest had worked out extremely well and, having reportedly schooled like a natural, including over fences, it was no surprise to see him made a red-hot favourite, with the step up to 2m4f not expected to be a bother. Despite having taken a fierce hold for the first part of the race, he jumped well and his tank was still full as he charged ahead three out, easing clear to win as he pleased. Colin Tizzard, who said he had him straight for this reappearance, admitted to being relieved that this first run was out of the way and will now step him up in grade, with races from 2m–2m4f coming under consideration.

He is favourite for both the Supreme Novices' and Neptune at next year's Festival, but judging from his trainer's post-race inter- view, the Champion Hurdle, for which he's a 33-1 shot, is by no means out of the equation. It's likely he'll be out again soon, possi- bly at Cheltenham's Open meeting next month.

As Colin Tizzard had suggested, it would be Cheltenham and its Old course, over which Cue Card had been so magnificent in March, that the horse would return for his second start over hurdles.

It was decided to drop him in trip for the Grade 2 Sharp Novices' Hurdle over two miles and half a furlong, the exact same distance he had covered in the Champion Bumper.

"He has loads of pace and the only reason we stepped him up in trip at Aintree was because it looked such an easy starting point," said the trainer, who watched on as his flagbearer sought to justify 8-13 market leadership.

He duly justified those odds rather well.

If something looks too good to be true, so the saying goes, it usually is, but Cue Card, a ridiculously easy winner of the Weatherbys Champion Bumper and now unbeaten in four starts, might just be the exception.

Despite pulling hard, he had been a comfortable winner at Aintree last month on his hurdling debut. This time he was taking a big step up in class against seven previous winners in the Grade 2 Cheltenham Collection Sharp Novices' Hurdle,

AINTREE
EBF Bestway 'National Hunt'
Novices' Hurdle

CHELTENHAM
Cheltenham Collection
Sharp Novices' Hurdle

2009-10				2010-11					2011-12					2012-13					2013-14			
JAN	FEB	MAR	APR	NOV	DEC	JAN	FEB	MAR	APR	NOV	DEC	JAN	FEB	MAR	APR	NOV	DEC	JAN	FEB	MAR	APR	NOV	DEC	JAN	FEB

yet he won so impressively he is now no bigger than 3-1 for the Supreme Novices' Hurdle, and just 7-4 with Paddy Power.

We saw last season with Dunguib, another eye-catching Champion Bumper winner, the folly of taking short odds in a race like that – and we should remember that a shot at the Champion Hurdle has not been ruled out for Cue Card, although trainer Colin Tizzard will not discuss it seriously until Christmas – but there is no question the youngster is a rare talent.

After he had beaten the highly regarded Dunraven Storm by eight lengths – just pushed out, for educational purposes – Tizzard said: "It was everything we hoped for. It was a completely different race to last time, as it was a fast-run two miles, but he jumped well and stayed up the hill.

"He settled today, too. At Aintree the only negative was he pulled too hard. We'll have to mind him a bit now. He may only run once more before March."

Cue Card has now not been troubled in four racecourse appearances, but Tizzard's son Joe, his regular partner, is well aware there are much tougher assignments ahead and so was at pains to teach him as much as possible here.

He said: "They went a real good gallop and he settled particularly well. He came straight back on the bridle after I slapped him down the neck three out. I squeezed him so he'd attack the last, as races won't always be that easy, and then I pushed him out to the line as I wanted him to learn – come March there might be something to trouble him. You don't want to go to the festival without experience."

Revealingly, Tizzard added: "I still haven't had to hit him behind the saddle. He might take off if I did. He's a special horse and we are lucky to have him." (Lee Mottershead)

RACING POST ANALYSIS: All eyes were again on Cue Card, returning to the scene of his devastating Champion Bumper victory, and the good pace set by Irish raider Ballyadam Brook enabled him to settle considerably better than he had done on his hurdles debut at Aintree, when still managing to run out an easy winner.

> He's a special horse and we're lucky to have him"
>
> **JOE TIZZARD**

2014-15   2015-16   2016-17   2017-18

MAR | APR | NOV | DEC | JAN | FEB | MAR | APR | NOV | DEC | JAN | FEB | MAR | APR | NOV | DEC | JAN | FEB | MAR | APR | NOV | DEC | JAN | FEB | MAR | APR

Keen not to allow main market rival Dunraven Storm too much of a start, Joe Tizzard kept him within a few lengths throughout, and a quick jump two out, when the runner-up blundered, handed him the advantage. He just had to be squeezed to assert coming to the last and, as one would have expected, he stormed clear up the hill. Although he clearly possesses a lot of speed, there's little doubt his future lies over further, and the Neptune would seem the more sensible long-term target, being a race that goes to the best horse a high percentage of the time, whereas that isn't the case in the Supreme Novices', where there's always the danger he'll be done for speed by an ex-Flat racer. However, as was the case after Aintree, Colin Tizzard hinted the Champion Hurdle is very much an option, and we'll no doubt learn more again after his next appearance around Christmas time.

It seemed nigh on certain that Cue Card would feel a little warmth behind the saddle on his next outing, for it was decided to raise him significantly in class.

Up to now, Cue Card had been competing against his contemporaries in the form of either bumper performers or fellow novices. However, such had been the impression made in the opening two starts of his campaign, he was earmarked for one of the winter's leading Champion Hurdle trials, Cheltenham's StanJames.com International Hurdle.

This was an altogether stiffer sort of test, as evidenced by the fact that Cue Card was not sent off favourite. Yet it was also evidence of his towering reputation that he very nearly did go off favourite. Bookmakers returned him at 15-8, just behind 7-4 shot Menorah – also twice at that point a Cheltenham winner having landed the 2010 Supreme Novices' Hurdle and Greatwood Handicap Hurdle – and just in front of 5-2 fancy Silviniaco Conti, a wide-margin winner of the Grade 2 Ascot Hurdle leading into the International.

Silviniaco Conti – who would continue to play a prominent part in Cue Card's racing life – was this time beaten. So was Cue Card, but although defeated, he was far from disgraced.

From out of the big three emerged a potentially great one.

CHELTENHAM
Cheltenham Collection
Sharp Novices' Hurdle

CHELTENHAM
StanJames.com International Hurdle

Even those closest to Menorah had no expectation of seeing him do what he so brilliantly did yesterday, but then the Menorah they admired here was altogether different to the one we had all known before. A slicker, faster, better Menorah surged to the most devastating of victories in the StanJames. com International Hurdle, producing a performance that most observers agreed makes him the one to beat come the day of reckoning in March.

This was a race in which no bubbles were burst.

The exceptional novice Cue Card and the equally exciting Silviniaco Conti parted company with unbeaten records, but in defeat nothing was lost, for the vanquished were sunk by a victor who raised his game to an unexpectedly high level, one that persuaded most bookmakers to make him favourite for the Stan James Champion Hurdle.

Joe Tizzard said his mount had delivered "clearly the best run of his life".

Father Colin deferred a decision on his stable star's festival target, but conceded his great bay hope had been "beaten by a better horse on the day".

He added: "The winner came by him in four strides, but our horse has found his barometer and it's not too bad. Menorah must be a good horse."

Over the years that followed, Menorah confirmed himself to be a very good horse, albeit one who perhaps never reached the heights that might have been expected on that December afternoon.

When reflecting on Cue Card's first taste of not being first, Colin Tizzard suggested he may have been a couple of strong gallops short of being at full fitness. He very quickly vowed to keep the horse fresh for the Cheltenham Festival, to which he would head without another outing.

As 2010 turned into 2011, any thoughts of going for the Champion Hurdle evaporated. For that race, Cue Card was then a 33-1 shot. For the Supreme Novices' Hurdle, the championship prize that opens racing's most eagerly awaited meeting, he was the 5-2 favourite.

There was clearly good reason to look forward. It was also a good time to look back, as Rodney Masters did when telling Cue Card's story – so far.

Two offers were made for Cue Card in recent weeks. Without hesitation, Bob and Jean Bishop politely rejected both overtures, explaining they have no intention of renouncing their long-set policy of being buyers, not sellers. Nothing will prise Cue Card away from them.

Bob Bishop, a former Lloyd's of London employee and ex-deputy chairman of Crystal Palace FC, declined to reveal the source of the submissions, or how much was on the table, but we can surmise they were well-known names proffering substantial sums.

Cue Card is a top-priced 5-2 for the Stan James Supreme Novices' Hurdle. For the time being at least, the festival's opening race is his intended target, although the Bishops and trainer Colin Tizzard agree the door will remain ajar to the Champion Hurdle and that door may be pushed wide enough for Cue Card to squeeze through in the eventuality of a leading contender or two defecting.

THE EARLY DAYS

By King's Theatre out of Wicked Crack, a six-time winner who led the charge when falling at the first fence in Bindaree's 2002 Grand National, Cue Card was bred near Newport in South Wales by Rowland Crellin. As a yearling he was consigned, on Crellin's behalf, by Richard and Sally Aston's Goldford Stud to the 2007 Tattersalls Ireland February National Hunt Sale. He was bought for Grahame and Diana Whateley for €75,000 via agent Aiden Murphy.

Richard Aston: "He was a beautiful-looking foal, a perfect athlete and everything you'd look for in a store horse. There was so much class about him; that tends to be a characteristic of King's Theatre's stock. As Wicked Crack came from one of those solid staying jumping families, you'd look at the pedi-

> " **He was a beautiful-looking foal, a perfect athlete and everything you'd look for in a store horse"**
>
> **RICHARD ASTON**

gree page and not believe he'd come to hand as quickly as he did, showing such a high level of ability at such an early age. It must augur extremely well."

Aiden Murphy: "He was a fine-looking youngster with a nice outlook. His dam wasn't black type, but she was a good, tough mare for Eddie Hales and the sire was making a name for himself. After the sale, Cue Card came to our farm at Stratford-upon-Avon."

With the Whateleys deciding on a change of policy, with their focus more on horses with form rather than stores, the unbroken Cue Card was back at the Astons' Goldford Stud near Malpas in Cheshire for the six weeks prior to being dispatched to the 2009 Tattersalls Ireland Derby Sale. With the recession biting deep by then, he was sold for €23,000 less than he had made as a yearling.

Aston: "He was just a bigger model of before, with all the same attributes. There was a loss on the deal, which was a shame, but it wasn't a reflection on the horse, simply the depressed state of the market."

Meanwhile, shortly before the Derby Sale, in Bexhill-on-Sea in East Sussex, the Bishops were studying the sale catalogue and Jean had marked one page for special attention.

Bob Bishop: "We go to the Derby Sale every summer. Jean had ringed Cue Card's pedigree and lot number. We went to see him the night before the sale. There wasn't anyone else about, but then we saw Sally Aston leading a horse out of block A. We both remarked what a magnificent-looking horse and, of course, it turned out to be Cue Card. We were so taken by him we didn't look at any others. We drove back to the hotel and bumped into Colin and Pauline Tizzard. We suggested that first thing next morning they take a look at lot 116. They liked him immediately. I know it sounds daft, but it was almost as if it was meant to be. He went straight to Rodi Greene's yard near Wellington in Somerset to be broken in."

Rodi Greene: "He was the easiest of pupils with a most likeable character. He did everything right from the first day.

He was the easiest of pupils with a most likeable character. He did everything right from the first day"

RODI GREENE

Although at that stage it was impossible to tell how good he was going to be, he had so much scope and there was plenty of evidence that he'd be the most willing of characters. He was here for three weeks. From then on I was forever asking Colin Tizzard as to when the King's Theatre would run."

Colin Tizzard: "I was impressed with him at the Derby Sale. He was one of those wonderful loose movers with a big eye. His pedigree was everything I'd look for. Often we buy stores, but when I saw him I thought we could win a race sooner rather than later. He was cantering and then we gave him his first bit of work. He was brilliant. That's rare because many horses in their first bit of work don't go any faster than before. It was then that we knew."

Bishop: "After a few weeks, Colin rang and said he reckoned this one could be a bit special. He was declared to run in a bumper at Exeter in December and we made the five-and-a-half-hour journey down to see him. Unfortunately for us fog closed in and the final race of the day was abandoned. It could have been a blessing, though, with the extra few weeks until his first race giving him more time."

THE FIRST RACE

Fontwell, January 2010. A marginal drifter in the market, Cue Card wins a soft-ground bumper over 1m5½f by six lengths. The runner-up and fourth home were to endorse the form with wins next time. The Racing Post analysis read: "He made smooth headway when things began to get serious and responded strongly when asked to seal the race. He eventually came right away, looking suited by the soft ground, and looks a very nice prospect."

Bishop: "Colin told us he'd been working so well it would take a good one to beat him. Afterwards, as we walked to the winner's enclosure, Colin turned to me and asked, 'Where should we go next?' When I replied the festival bumper, he said he'd been thinking the same."

Tizzard: "I told everyone who'd listen that he'd win, although all his work had been done on our woodchip and nowhere else. We'd not taken him off the farm to gallop. Sometimes they can make fools of you in their first race."

AND SO TO CHELTENHAM

A 40-1 shot for the Weatherbys Champion Bumper, Cue Card darts clear up the hill under Joe Tizzard to win by eight lengths.

The Racing Post close-up comment read: "Took keen hold, held up well in rear, scythed through field from 5f out, tracked leader over 2f out and still cruising, led over 1f out, hung left briefly but romped clear."

The execution of the win was likened to Dunguib's the previous season, but Cue Card was the first four-year-old to take the race since Dato Star in 1995.

Bishop: "A fortnight before the race, Colin was enthusing about him so much I said let's not talk about him again until the race and then we'll let the horse do the talking.

"Accordingly, during that period he'd ring about our other horses and at the end of every conversation he'd simply mention that Cue Card was doing all right. On the day when Cue Card was in the paddock, Claude Charlet came up and told me I was mad for running a four-year-old in the Champion Bumper. Afterwards Claude conceded he was wrong."

Tizzard: "It was stunning. I couldn't believe what I was watching. An hour before the race I'd been very concerned he'd pull too hard. I told Joe to sit in and not to be in the first half-dozen, which had been our original plan. About halfway Joe pulled out and Cue Card quickened. Then he quickened again up the hill."

Murphy: "It was astonishing that in nine months he went from the Derby Sale, unbroken, to winning the festival's Champion Bumper. One shouldn't underestimate that achievement. He's bred to stay and it's to his credit he has shown such speed, with a turn of foot, over two miles. He's such a lovely character, too."

"

He was one of those wonderful loose movers with a big eye. His pedigree was everything I'd look for"

COLIN TIZZARD

> **"**
>
> He'd been a good jumper from his first day on our schooling ground"
>
> **COLIN TIZZARD**

THE SWITCH TO JUMPING

Aintree, October 2010. Over 2m4f and 11 flights, Cue Card overwhelms Dear Sam and Mr Moonshine, who was to win at Huntingdon in January. The Racing Post comment-in-running read: "Raced keenly, held up, not fluent four out, smooth headway soon after, upsides with big jump three out, soon led on bit, clear when jumped left last, very easily."

Tizzard: "He'd been a good jumper from his first day on our schooling ground. He pulled hard but outclassed them. It was a perfect start."

Cheltenham, November 2010. Over 2m½f and eight flights. Apart from a mistake at the third, it was another trouble-free round to beat Dunraven Storm, whose only previous defeat in five starts was in Cue Card's festival bumper. However, Dunraven Storm failed to enhance the form, finishing last of four when 1-2 favourite on his only subsequent start.

Tizzard: "As he'd pulled at Aintree, we thought the extra pace over two would make him an easier ride. It was never a case of not believing he'd stay because we knew he would."

THE FIRST DEFEAT

Cheltenham, December 2010. The Whateley-owned Menorah, 7-4 favourite, beats the former Whateley-owned Cue Card, 15-8, by four and a half lengths. In third, half a length away, is Silviniaco Conti and doubters of the form will point to his 24-length defeat by Mille Chief next time in Wincanton's Grade 2 Kingwell Hurdle.

Bishop: "He'd missed quite a bit of work due to the bad weather. In the ten days prior to the race he didn't do as much as he normally would before a run. It showed in the race that he was that bit short. However, by saying that I don't want to take anything away from Menorah."

Tizzard: "I wasn't disappointed at being beaten by Menorah, who may well win the Champion, although that day a few finished closer to us than I'd expected. The explanation was that he'd had an interrupted preparation. He'd looked better

Cue Card and Joe Tizzard are poetry
in motion as they clear the final flight
at Aintree in October 2010 to make
a winning debut over hurdles

than ever but had put on a bit of weight; when he's fully fit he's quite angular. Under the circumstances, it was a really good performance. I've always thought that one day we'd again take on Menorah."

Bishop: "We said the Supreme and that's our first choice unless anything untoward happens to the top names in the Champion. It was a very close decision for us. We concluded that as he's a novice he should remain in novice company."

Tizzard: "Being a novice, the Supreme was the obvious objective, but it wouldn't take too much change to the shape of the Champion for us to reconsider. If three or four of the top ones come out, a swap is entirely possible. A 12- or 14-runner Champion would be tempting rather than a 22-runner race. We're open-minded about it. In the Supreme he's obviously the one to beat on all known form, but there's always the risk of one lurking in the wings. Such is the nature of racing, sometimes you have to take the opportunities when they come your way."

AND BACK TO CHELTENHAM

Tizzard: "He'll have a racecourse gallop in the next day or two at Exeter or Wincanton, or perhaps at Newbury on Sunday. He'll not be going flat out, just a half-pace over two miles."

Tizzard chose Wincanton for that gallop. "He was brilliant," said the trainer. In the Stan James Supreme Novices' Hurdle, for which he began galloping as 7-4 favourite, he was not.

Graham Dench was reporting as Cue Card managed fourth behind Al Ferof, the grey who 12 months earlier had been eight lengths his inferior when second in the Champion Bumper.

Ruby Walsh enjoyed the festival start that he can scarcely have dreamed of during that long dark winter on the sidelines when producing Al Ferof from off the pace to land a famous victory.

It was a nightmare start for many punters, however, for long-time ante-post favourite Cue Card, backed down to 7-4 on course after being laid heavily at 3-1 in the morning, finished only fourth.

Walsh had returned only 11 days previously from the double leg fracture he suffered at Down Royal in November and his comeback had suffered another brief setback when a last-flight fall at Naas last Wednesday left him needing stitches to his right eye.

Timing can be everything in racing and trainer Paul Nicholls revealed it was only on Saturday, just hours before Walsh got back on the scoreboard at Sandown, that Al Ferof pleased him for the first time this season.

Colin Tizzard pictured at home with Cue Card – his pride and joy

CHELTENHAM
Stan James Supreme
Novices' Hurdle

He said: "Saturday was the first time he's worked and I've thought 'wow'. I thought he'd run well, and remember he was giving weight away when he was second to Cue Card here in the bumper."

Connections of Cue Card could offer no real excuse. A year on, the runaway winner of the 2010 Weatherbys Champion Bumper looked short of the requisite finishing speed and was already getting the worse of a battle for the lead with Sprinter Sacre turning for home.

Trainer Colin Tizzard said: "He ran well but not so well as the first three. We can't make any excuses.

"He got there as easy as any horse but we have been beaten. He'll be better over fences, but that's for another day.

"There has been so much hype about this horse but I'm not disappointed at all. I'm just glad he has come back safe and sound."

Jockey Joe Tizzard added: "I'm not going to make excuses as I haven't got any. We were beaten fair and square."

At Aintree the following month, he was beaten fair and square again. Sent back to the track where he had produced such a striking display the previous October, Cue Card was also returned to the same distance he won over that afternoon.

However, the aim of gaining some compensation for the festival reverse in the John Smith's Mersey Novices' Hurdle did not reap winning dividends. This time Cue Card, the 5-2 favourite, advanced to second, but a long 13 lengths behind the Supreme second Spirit Son, a hugely exciting racehorse who was unable to race again after this victory.

Spirit Son may be another ace in the pack of high-class hurdlers that Nicky Henderson has to shuffle each season, as he signed off his novice career with a consolation Grade 2 win in the John Smith's Mersey Novices' Hurdle.

The five-year-old may have beaten the hyped leader of the novice pack Cue Card when second in the 2m Grade 1

> **"**
> I'm just glad he's come back safe and sound'"
> **COLIN TIZZARD**

CHELTENHAM
Stan James Supreme
Novices' Hurdle

AINTREE
John Smith's Mersey Novices' Hurdle

Supreme Novices' at Cheltenham, but was still second-best in the betting for the rematch over an extra half-mile.

Punters knew their fate turning into the straight, where Barry Geraghty let Spirit Son stride on and a niggled-along Cue Card could not take up the chase and toiled home 13 lengths adrift.

The former Champion Bumper winner has had the bubble surrounding last season's exploits well and truly pricked. Trainer Colin Tizzard was disappointed Cue Card needed nudging along to make ground to get in a challenge before being left behind in a slowly run race.

He said: "I thought he could sit and travel and pick them up. I was surprised we had to wake him up on the bottom bend to challenge. He'll go novice chasing next season." (Bruce Jackson)

A stint over hurdles that started on a high ended in dejection. There had been peaks and there had been troughs. The rest of Cue Card's career would continue in the same vein.

2
FESTIVAL GLORY

Previous spread: joy unconfined as Cue Card and Joe Tizzard are led into the winner's enclosure after winning the Ryanair Chase in March 2013

ONE PLACE in front of Cue Card in the Supreme Novices' Hurdle was a horse who would, like Cue Card himself, turn out to be much better over fences than he had been over hurdles. More than that, plenty would argue Sprinter Sacre was better than any horse who has ever jumped a fence, save for the incomparable Arkle.

It was not only in the Supreme that Sprinter Sacre and Cue Card clapped eyes on each other.

Indeed, over the following two seasons the former would play a significant part in the career of the latter, both in terms of where Cue Card finished in his races and in which races he actually lined up.

At the start of the 2011–12 season, both horses ranked as amongst the most promising individuals switching from hurdles to fences. Consideration had been given to extending Cue Card's life in the former discipline, but while Colin Tizzard briefly raised the option of aiming towards the Ladbrokes World Hurdle, reigning champion Big Buck's appeared to be a rare force in the long-distance division.

So it was, then, that Cue Card was sent in early October to Chepstow. Three opponents took him on in the two-mile-three-and-a-half-furlong novice chase, including the Paul Nicholls-trained Silviniaco Conti, who the previous December had passed the judge half a length behind Cue Card in the International Hurdle.

As Rodney Masters saw, the five-year-old posted a highly encouraging introduction to his new job.

It augured well for future assignments when Cue Card served up the aces on all fronts on his chasing debut.

Clever enough to get himself out of trouble when getting in too tight to the occasional fence down the back straight, the 10-11 favourite jumped brilliantly at a quicker tempo once turning for home and already had matters under control when showboating with a fast and accurate leap at the final fence.

"These cat-and-mouse races are never easy but this is some horse," said Colin Tizzard after the three-and-a-half-length win over Micheal Flips.

"It was no bad thing he got in deep to a fence or two because he was very safe the way he dealt with it."

> **"**
> These cat-and-mouse races are never easy but this is some horse"
> **COLIN TIZZARD**

CHEPSTOW
Bet At bluesq.com On Your
Mobile Novices' Chase

Tizzard has no immediate next stopping point in mind, but feels Cue Card will be a better horse this winter than last.

"He had quite a hard time of it at the end of last season and I'm not sure he was quite right. He has strengthened up and is more relaxed."

Joe Tizzard said the original plan was not to make the running, but none of his three rivals wanted to lead.

"He had his ears pricked all the way and thoroughly enjoyed himself. The quicker he went the better he jumped. He was brilliant at the last."

Cue Card makes a winning debut over fences at Chepstow in October 2011

Bob Bishop, husband of owner Jean Bishop, said they were more relaxed after watching Cue Card school on Wednesday. "He was very good, just as Colin had told us. That's the thing with Colin, he always tells us the truth."

RACING POST ANALYSIS: There wasn't much pace on, which wouldn't really have suited either of the 'big' two, but as the race panned out, it played best to the strengths of Cue Card, who, having been allowed to stride, saw his superior pace, and possibly class, carry him clear down the straight. His jumping was novicey on occasions, but good when it needed to be, and it's likely he'll improve quite a bit for the match practice. Although not living up to expectations for some last season, he still regularly performed to a high level, and it's probable the Supreme, in which he was a beaten favourite, was a strong renewal. Connections couldn't have wished for a better start to his season and the 2m novice chase at Cheltenham's Open meeting will presumably be on his schedule, with the Arkle, for which he's a top-priced 16-1, no doubt the long-term aim.

Cue Card finished the race as short as 10-1 for the Racing Post Arkle Chase. It was, however, far from guaranteed the Arkle would be his Cheltenham Festival target. A new two-and-a-half-mile novice chase had been introduced at the fixture the previous season, while a further option was the novices' Gold Cup, the three-mile RSA Chase, about which Colin Tizzard mused: "You can just see him going round there on the bridle, quickening up off the last bend and leaving them for dead."

That thought, though, was qualified by another.

"There is an awful long way to go and I don't know what trip he really wants," added the trainer. "He could be effective from two miles to three, but I can't see any point in going up to three miles yet as he has so much pace."

A decision was taken to stay at roughly the same trip, with Cue Card pointed to Cheltenham's November meeting for a two-and-a-half-mile novice chase, which took place at a time when the Tizzard yard was stuck in a losing sequence of 33 runners over five weeks.

"

He was very good, just as Colin had told us. That's the thing with Colin, he always tells us the truth"

BOB BISHOP

CHEPSTOW
Bet At bluesq.com On Your Mobile Novices' Chase

CHELTENHAM
Steel Plate And Sections Novices' Chase

NEWBURY
Berkshire Novices' Chase

2009-10   2010-11   2011-12   2012-13   2013-14

JAN FEB MAR APR NOV DEC JAN FEB MAR APR NOV DEC JAN FEB MAR APR NOV DEC JAN FEB MAR APR NOV DEC JAN FEB

Cue Card was unable to help. Grands Crus was sent off 6-4 favourite thanks to his second in the previous season's World Hurdle. He won. Cue Card was sent off 7-4 second favourite. He failed to complete, unseating Joe Tizzard at the open ditch that follows the water jump.

It was a setback but a relatively minor one. Novice chases are contested by novice chasers who lack experience jumping fences in public. Aside from the blunder – one that gave his rider little chance of keeping the partnership intact – the Bishops' charge had jumped pleasingly. He therefore merited an early chance to get back on track.

The track he got back on was Newbury for the Grade 2 Berkshire Novices' Chase, again over two and a half miles. Once again he played second fiddle in the betting, this time trailing Nicky Henderson's Bobs Worth, who when last seen in March had won the Cheltenham Festival's Grade 1 Albert Bartlett Novices' Hurdle. The following March he would win the RSA Chase. Fast forward a further 12 months and Bobs Worth captured the most prestigious jumps prize of all, the Cheltenham Gold Cup.

As such, Cue Card – who on this occasion sported what became his customary sheepskin noseband for the first time – was facing an extremely talented racehorse.

Moreover, due to the race conditions he was required to concede 7lb. With hindsight, it was no disgrace to be beaten only a short head.

The frustration was that after holding a two-length lead at the final fence, and having looked the likely winner all the way up the home straight, he was headed for the only time in the race right on the line. As is often the case in such circumstances, some pointed figures at the man in the saddle. That man's father did not, as was evident in a Racing Post update one day after the narrow defeat.

Trainer Colin Tizzard yesterday leapt to the defence of his son Joe after he came in for criticism for the ride he gave Cue Card at Newbury on Friday.

The winner of the Champion Bumper at the Cheltenham Festival in 2010 was sent off the 2-1 second favourite for his third start over fences but was beaten a short head by favourite

> We all watched it and thought he was going to win but he got nabbed by a very good horse to whom he was trying to give 7lb"
>
> **COLIN TIZZARD**

Bobs Worth having been caught in the final stride after looking a certain winner on the run-in.

The five-year-old had made all the running up to that point and despite blundering four out, Joe Tizzard had taken a couple of looks over his shoulder before allowing his mount to pop the last fence, something the rider himself said might have made the difference.

However, the trainer said: "There has been a lot of talk that he should have won and could have won. For me Joe got him jumping beautifully and two out he looked like he was going to pull away and win by five.

"We all watched it and thought he was going to win but he got nabbed by a very good horse to whom he was trying to give 7lb."

For novice chase number four, Cue Card was asked to give 7lb to another high-class performer. This time it was For Non Stop, a neck second to Supreme winner Al Ferof in a Sandown Grade 1. The venue was once again Newbury, but the distance of the New Year's Eve event was the shortest Cue Card had hitherto tackled over fences.

Andrew King was in the Newbury press room as Cue Card resumed winning ways.

Following a succession of attempts at further, Cue Card's victory in the 2m2½f novice chase finally saw trainer Colin Tizzard conclude that the five-year-old's target at the Cheltenham Festival will be the Arkle Chase.

Although error-prone at times, Cue Card's jumping proved better than his three rivals, and in the end Joe Tizzard only had to drive him out after the final fence to outclass the Nick Williams-trained For Non Stop by four lengths.

Tizzard senior said: "It has become obvious the horse is a spring-heeled two-miler, so with that in mind we will now be happy to go down the Arkle route. We have been trying to get him to stay further and it has not worked."

NEWBURY
Berkshire Novices' Chase

NEWBURY
Betfred Goals Galore
Novices' Chase

RACING POST ANALYSIS: Cue Card, touched off by Bobs Worth over 2m4f here last time, went off in front and raced with enthusiasm. His jumping held up pretty well, and he went clear after three out as his rivals faltered. He tended to idle on the run-in but was always going to hold on. This was a fine effort giving weight to the second and it will be interesting to see where he goes next, although his rider is convinced he is an ideal Arkle type.

Cue Card gets back on the winning trail at Newbury on New Year's Eve 2011 after two defeats

2014-15 2015-16 2016-17 2017-18

MAR APR NOV DEC JAN FEB MAR APR NOV DEC JAN FEB MAR APR NOV DEC JAN FEB MAR APR NOV DEC JAN FEB MAR APR

In an ideal world, Cue Card would have run once more before the festival. That run was intended to be against senior opposition in Newbury's Game Spirit Chase. Had he run in that race it is entirely possible Cue Card would have swerved the Arkle, for the Game Spirit was the scene of a remarkable performance.

Sprinter Sacre – who had so far been successful in novice chases at Doncaster and Kempton – won the Game Spirit by six lengths without coming off the bridle. It was an astonishing exhibition, one that prompted Henderson to observe: "He is something else. It's a bit scary really."

Had Cue Card met Sprinter Sacre at Newbury it is long odds-on he would have come off second best and therefore been rerouted to the JLT at Cheltenham. Instead, he was forced out of the Game Spirit after knocking a joint and confirmed a runner in the Arkle.

Connections hoped his proven stamina over two and a half miles would provide him with a trump card over two miles. Attempting to exploit that, Joe Tizzard fired Cue Card into an early lead. That lead was maintained for the first half of the race. For the rest of the race, Sprinter Sacre was in complete control and sauntered to success.

Even so, Cue Card was the only one to get close to the winner, and with old foes Menorah and Al Ferof 22 lengths and 25 and a quarter lengths behind him, the Arkle second had never run a finer race.

Seven lengths separated Sprinter Sacre and Cue Card. Joe Tizzard described himself as "over the moon", but that upbeat mood dipped when a minor setback meant Aintree came and went without Cue Card. His first season over fences was over.

As the Flat-filled summer began to give way to autumn and people's thoughts started returning towards racing's top jumpers, the Tizzards and Bishops set out a provisional plan for Cue Card in which the pivot point was Boxing Day and Kempton's King George VI Chase. But how to get there?

Among the races considered were the Charlie Hall Chase at Wetherby and a £100,000 handicap held at Ascot the same day. Either contest would have led to Cue Card running over three miles for the first time. That day would have to wait, for selected instead

CHELTENHAM
Racing Post Arkle Challenge
Trophy Chase

EXETER
sportingbet Haldon Gold Cup Chase

2009-10					2010-11					2011-12					2012-13					2013-14			
JAN	FEB	MAR	APR	NOV	DEC	JAN	FEB	MAR	APR	NOV	DEC	JAN	FEB	MAR	APR	NOV	DEC	JAN	FEB	MAR	APR	NOV	DEC	JAN	FEB

was the biggest race in Exeter's calendar, the Haldon Gold Cup, a limited handicap over two miles one and a half furlongs.

Despite being slammed by Cue Card in the Arkle, Menorah had to shoulder 3lb more.

Off a rating of 157, the pride of Dorset appeared to be treated rather leniently. Aided by a slick jumping display, he showed that to be the case, storming to a huge success, as seen by Rodney Masters.

After Cue Card blitzed to a 26-length solo charge at Exeter, most of the debrief talk was of a Boxing Day challenge for the King George Vl Chase, for which he has been cut to 10-1 (from 20) by the sponsors William Hill.

But part-owner Bob Bishop insisted Cue Card, who is as short as 8-1 for the Kempton showpiece with Paddy Power,

Cue Card is no match for the brilliant Sprinter Sacre in the 2012 Arkle Chase at Cheltenham

2014-15   2015-16   2016-17   2017-18

MAR | APR | NOV | DEC | JAN | FEB | MAR | APR | NOV | DEC | JAN | FEB | MAR | APR | NOV | DEC | JAN | FEB | MAR | APR | NOV | DEC | JAN | FEB | MAR | APR

would not shy away from another showdown at some stage with his Arkle conqueror Sprinter Sacre.

Paul Nicholls, trainer of runner-up Edgardo Sol, was one of the first to congratulate Bishop and his wife Jean after Cue Card's runaway romp, the fourth successive occasion he has won on his seasonal debut.

What Nicholls then said gave Bishop food for thought.

"Paul mentioned that Cue Card had shown such speed and asked why would we want to take him away from two miles," he said.

"While Sprinter Sacre beat us into second in the Arkle last season, I certainly wouldn't rule out a rematch. I've never run away from anything in my life and I wouldn't run away from taking on Sprinter Sacre again."

Bishop, former deputy chairman of Crystal Palace FC, added: "While Sprinter Sacre may well have improved, so has our horse. He has grown up. We've had horses for 26 years but this is one of our best days. It makes up for the bad ones, and we've had quite a few of those."

Jockey Joe Tizzard was non-committal when asked what he thought was the winner's optimum trip.

He said: "It's so difficult to say. This was a fabulous run and he has shown such speed. I never had an anxious moment. If we step up to three miles, the King George would definitely be the race for him. I'm sure Kempton will suit him."

It was the jockey's idea to head for yesterday's race. His father Colin – who laughed that he "would've thought about it soon enough though" – was thrilled with Cue Card's performance.

He said: "That was fantastic, to win by so far. He was faultless. The way he won raises the question as to whether we need to go up to three miles and we've got some thinking to do.

"However, I expect we'll aim for the King George because Kempton would be ideal over three miles. He'll have a run before, perhaps the Peterborough Chase, but we'll talk about

> **"**
> He's less fizzy than he was. As a three-year-old he'd jump out of the paddock at home, but he has grown up"
>
> **COLIN TIZZARD**

EXETER
sportingbet Haldon
Gold Cup Chase

| 2009-10 | | | | 2010-11 | | | | | 2011-12 | | | | | 2012-13 | | | | | 2013-14 | | | |
| JAN | FEB | MAR | APR | NOV | DEC | JAN | FEB | MAR | APR | NOV | DEC | JAN | FEB | MAR | APR | NOV | DEC | JAN | FEB | MAR | APR | NOV | DEC | JAN | FEB |

that. I made an entry for him this morning in the Betfair Chase, but I doubt he'd go there now."

Tizzard added that Cue Card, who showed admirable athleticism at the fences, and stretched his lead by two lengths with a fine leap at the open ditch, was more settled these days.

"He's less fizzy than he was. As a three-year-old he'd jump out of the paddock at home, but he has grown up," he said.

RACING POST ANALYSIS: There was an impressive winner, Cue Card, who'd been off since his fine second to Sprinter Sacre at Cheltenham, jumping boldly under a positive ride and surging clear

Cue Card makes an impressive reappearance in the Haldon Gold Cup at Exeter in November 2012

from the first in the straight. He looked best at the weights and the race worked out nicely, with Joe Tizzard able to get a breather into him leaving the back, and on this evidence he's taken a step forward from last year, although it's worth bearing in mind neither the second nor third were seen to best effect.

A delighted Joe and Colin Tizzard with Cue Card in the winner's enclosure after the Haldon Gold Cup

Contrary to what Colin Tizzard said at Exeter, Cue Card was not given another run before the King George.

Instead he went directly to Kempton, where the 2012 field for the Christmas classic was headed by Long Run, a previous winner of both that race and the Gold Cup.

It was said that Cue Card had never been better. Unfortunately, he had certainly jumped better than he did in his first assault on the King George. Stamina was the big question hanging over him but, truth be told, this turned out to be a race in which his capacity to stay three miles could not properly be tested.

EXETER
sportingbet Haldon
Gold Cup Chase

KEMPTON
William Hill King George
VI Chase

ASCOT
Betfair Ascot Chase

2009–10   2010–11   2011–12   2012–13   2013–14
JAN FEB MAR APR NOV DEC JAN FEB MAR APR NOV DEC JAN FEB MAR APR NOV DEC JAN FEB MAR APR NOV DEC JAN FEB

On horribly heavy ground, Cue Card got the first fence horribly wrong, hitting it hard and almost headbutting the turf. The second fence then got a similar thwack. This was not going well, although the 5-1 shot appeared to be going very well when cruising into contention approaching the fourth-last fence. Yet when push came to shove, the cupboard was bare. Cue Card passed the post a very weary horse in a very distant fifth.

Joe Tizzard said: "He missed the first and then never got home in the ground. I knew he was beaten four out and he was a tired horse over the last three fences.

"I'm not saying we'll drop him back to two miles but he has got so much toe that we'll probably look at the Ryanair Chase."

Initial Cheltenham Festival entries were revealed early in the new year. When they came out, Cue Card appeared amongst the possible runners for the Ryanair and Champion Chase but not the Gold Cup.

The attractiveness of the Ryanair was obvious, not least because Sprinter Sacre was a red-hot market leader for the Champion Chase. There was, nonetheless, one person in the Cue Card camp not completely terrified of the big, black, beautiful beast.

Speaking a few days before Cue Card trialled for Cheltenham in the Grade 1 Ascot Chase, Bob Bishop said: "Which race he runs in at Cheltenham will depend on how he gets on at Ascot. I don't mind either way. I wouldn't be put off running in the Champion Chase because of Sprinter Sacre – why run away from one horse?"

At Ascot on February 16, one horse finished upwards of six lengths clear of all his rivals. Here's what I wrote on the day.

The Tizzards are sure in the knowledge that in their hand is a seriously strong card; knowing when to play that trump is a question still to be answered.

To bypass a Cheltenham Festival prize for which you are favourite would be bold, perhaps even reckless, but it is a possibility that remains a daring option for the connections of Cue Card following his six-length defeat of an arguably unlucky Captain Chris in Ascot's most valuable jumps race.

> **"**
> I'm not saying we'll drop him back to two miles, but he's got so much toe that we'll probably look at the Ryanair Chase"
>
> **JOE TIZZARD**

2014-15 2015-16 2016-17 2017-18

MAR | APR | NOV | DEC | JAN | FEB | MAR | APR | NOV | DEC | JAN | FEB | MAR | APR | NOV | DEC | JAN | FEB | MAR | APR | NOV | DEC | JAN | FEB | MAR | APR

With a performance far removed from his lacklustre Boxing Day effort at Kempton, Cue Card soared right back to his best as he made the most of a penultimate-fence error by Captain Chris to land a Betfair Ascot Chase, in which last season's Champion Chase winner Finian's Rainbow trailed in a weary last.

Altogether different was the display of front-running by Cue Card, now as short as 3-1 favourite for the Ryanair Chase but between 7-1 and 14-1 to exact revenge on his Arkle conqueror Sprinter Sacre in the two-mile championship.

"He is a damned good horse and Joe said he still had two or three more gears left when Captain Chris made his mistake," said trainer Colin Tizzard.

"We'll leave it until the last minute but he is favourite for the Ryanair and 10-1 for the Queen Mother. That tells its own story, but if Sprinter Sacre wasn't in the Champion Chase it would be very tempting."

Sure to be involved in the decision is his rider, who said: "He was brilliant today and got the trip very well on ground that was a little bit dead. It's hard to say what would have happened if Captain Chris hadn't made his mistake, but Dickie [Johnson] had to work to get to me and I was just picking up.

"He had his own way out in front and that's the way to ride him. I probably should have popped him out in front in the King George but it was his first time over three miles and it didn't seem the right thing to do."

Three and a quarter miles will be next for the King George runner-up Captain Chris, who heads to the Betfred Cheltenham Gold Cup unchanged at 20-1 with the sponsor.

For Cue Card, there are now two options. The man who must decide is owner Bob Bishop – and his heart is telling him to go against the flow.

"We thought he wasn't right for the King George and this proved it," said Bishop. "We would like to go for the Queen Mother but I think my family might try to sway me towards the Ryanair. I'm not easily swayed, though."

3.50   Betfair Ascot Chase Grade
[OFF 3.51]   1 Class 1   17 fences 2m5½f
For: 5-y-o and up **1st £34,405** 2nd £31,800 3rd £15,915 4th £7,950 5th £3,999 6th £1,995

1   **CUE CARD** 7 11-7 ....(165) **Joe Tizzard**
     b g by King's Theatre (IRE)–Wicked Crack (IRE) (King's Ride)
     (Colin Tizzard) made virtually off, mistake and stumbled 11th, 3
     lengths ahead when mistake 4 out, pressed next, still going well
     enough when headed and left clear 2 out, in no danger after [bets
     of £5,000-£2,000, £750-£300, £4,500-£2,000(x2), £1,800-£800,
     £900-£400, £800-£400]   [op 5/2] **15/8F**

2   6 **CAPTAIN CHRIS (IRE)** 9 11-7 t ..(169) Richard Johnson
     b g by King's Theatre (IRE)–Function Dream (IRE) (Strong Gale)
     (Philip Hobbs) tracked winner, closed 3 out, driven to lead 2 out
     but terrible blunder and lost all chance, held on for 2nd near finish
     [bets of £2,750-£1,000, £1,100-£400, £825-£300, £2,000-£800,
     £1,250-£500]   [op 9/4] **11/4**

3   1½ **GHIZAO (GER)** 9 11-7 ....(155) R Walsh
     [7½] b g by Tiger Hill (IRE)–Gliorosia (FR) (Bering)
     (Paul Nicholls) tracked leading trio, ridden and outpaced from 3
     out, 12 lengths behind leading pair 2 out, stayed on from last to
     take 3rd close home   [op 9/1] **12/1**

ASCOT
Betfair Ascot Chase

Cue Card puts in a mighty leap at the final fence in the 2013 Ascot Chase

Joe Tizzard pushes Cue Card out to record a first Grade 1 victory over fences

2014–15 2015–16 2016–17 2017–18

MAR | APR | NOV | DEC | JAN | FEB | MAR | APR | NOV | DEC | JAN | FEB | MAR | APR | NOV | DEC | JAN | FEB | MAR | APR | NOV | DEC | JAN | FEB | MAR | APR

Cue Card with his delighted connections in the Ascot winner's enclosure in February 2013

RACING POST ANALYSIS: It would have been an interesting finish between Cue Card and Captain Chris, with the latter looking set to take a narrow lead when diving at the second-last and losing any chance. The winner, who ended up around 20 lengths behind the runner-up when finishing very tired in the King George, enjoyed an uncontested lead but wasn't always fluent and one would fancy he'd have been outstayed, although he didn't exactly finish like a tired horse and post-race comments by his jockey suggests he had plenty left. This performance surely cements his place in the Ryanair and, given his fine record at the festival, he heads there with strong claims.

— ASCOT
Betfair Ascot Chase

Over the years that followed, master wordsmith Alastair Down would write plenty of pieces in which Cue Card was the central character. This was the first of them.

It would be hard to knock Cue Card off any shortlist of the most admirable horses in training and he cemented his place at the top of the Ryanair market when landing Ascot's Betfair Chase under Joe Tizzard, who is one of the few men to have stuck his head in a baling machine and emerge with his brain intact. Although just how intact jump jockeys' brains actually are remains a matter for some debate.

If you forgive Cue Card an uncharacteristically duff run in the swamp of the King George and one unseated as a novice chaser, the only time he has finished out of the first two in 15 races was when a close fourth to Al Ferof in the 2011 Supreme Novices' which is hardly shabby.

What is more he has punched above his weight from early on as he was one of just two four-year-olds in the 24-strong field for the festival bumper in 2010 when he danced up by eight lengths from future conqueror Al Ferof. He has always mixed it in the top class and his seven-length second to Sprinter Sacre in last year's Arkle was another rattling festival effort.

Trainer Colin Tizzard said simply: "He's a damn good horse and this was him today, whereas I don't think it was him in the King George where he was a bit flat."

It didn't help that Cue Card rooted the first two fences at Kempton and it wasn't exhibition stuff here with two palpable mistakes, the second four from home. And jumping proved decisive as Captain Chris had just headed him when making a total hash of the second-last, although for what it's worth, opinion on the press balcony was Cue Card would still have won.

In the run-up to Cheltenham the majority of trainers will insist they have a little bit to work on but Tizzard was peddling no such line.

> **"**
> He's a damn good horse and this was him today, whereas I don't think it was him in the King George where he was a bit flat"
>
> **COLIN TIZZARD**

"There wouldn't be a lot left to come," he said. "We've had a good three weeks with him and in the paddock he looked fit and hard.

"Joe said he had more gears but he sometimes says things like that. I am not entirely sure he wasn't stopping a bit late on but I'll have to have another look."

All the pundits in the stands regard it as a formality Cue Card will take the Ryanair route but none of them are called Tizzard or Bishop – the horse's enthusiastic owners.

There is no doubt Sprinter Sacre is a monster but there has always been huge belief in deepest Dorset in Cue Card and it would be no surprise if there were some vigorous discussion over a few pints of local bitter before the die is cast.

It is one of racing's oldest adages you "should never be afraid of one", although in all honesty if you are ever going to duck a single horse then you can be forgiven for making it Sprinter Sacre. Not for nothing is the second half of his name an anagram of Scare.

There is also the still emerging status of the Ryanair Chase to consider. It has fast established itself as a super race but, however much the great and good of Cheltenham may huff and puff in defending its growing reputation, there wouldn't be a racing fan from Wick to Woolacombe who thinks it has the prestige or pedigree of the Champion Chase. Some would say the Cue Card team would be insane to take on Sprinter Sacre, others might choose the word brave. Bonkers but brave.

Certainly Joe Tizzard made a telling point when he said Cue Card would not be granted a soft lead in the Ryanair and that "they wouldn't let him have things his own way".

They picked the Ryanair.

On the Wednesday of the festival, Sprinter Sacre annihilated the Champion Chase field, winning with ridiculous ease.

On the Thursday of the festival, Cue Card took his place in a race Colin Tizzard described as a "great opportunity" for his stable star.

"He looks beautiful, hard and fit," he said in the race preview.

ASCOT
Betfair Ascot Chase

CHELTENHAM
Ryanair Chase

2009-10					2010-11					2011-12					2012-13					2013-14			
JAN	FEB	MAR	APR	NOV	DEC	JAN	FEB	MAR	APR	NOV	DEC	JAN	FEB	MAR	APR	NOV	DEC	JAN	FEB	MAR	APR	NOV	DEC	JAN	FEB

He looked beautiful, hard and fit in the race itself. I know I certainly enjoyed watching him and then writing the words below.

By bowing down to the brilliance of an invincible foe, they allowed us to see the magnificence of their own animal. The connections of Cue Card were frightened of Sprinter Sacre and right to be so. Now, wherever their own horse goes, others will be scared.

Ever since the runaway winner of the 2010 Weatherbys Champion Bumper had claimed a second Grade 1 triumph at Ascot in February, a decision had needed to be made. To have faced Sprinter Sacre on Wednesday would have been brave but foolhardy. By purchasing a ticket to the Ryanair Chase, the families Tizzard and Bishop opted for a prize that lacks the prestige of the Sportingbet Queen Mother Champion Chase. But it is a championship race and, by slamming a top-class opponent by nine lengths, Cue Card put up a championship performance.

From start to finish he led, jumping boldly under Joe Tizzard, whose muscles had still to move when all those behind him were in trouble. Although pressed repeatedly, the seven-year-old answered every call, pulling impressively clear of fellow former festival winner First Lieutenant, who himself was well on top of third-placed For Non Stop. Riverside Theatre, the victor of 2012, could manage only fourth, while dual Ryanair winner Albertas Run was pulled up.

"I knew he was good, but I didn't think he was as good as that," said Bob Bishop, who owns Cue Card with wife Jean. Aside from the occasional blip – notably his below-par effort in the William Hill King George VI Chase – Cue Card has given the couple one high after another in a career directed by another couple, a father-and-son team who have become an increasingly potent force.

"I've always said he's the best I've ever had and the best I'll ever get," said trainer Colin Tizzard, who had been successful on Tuesday with Golden Chieftain.

> **"**
> I knew he was good, but I didn't think he was as good as that"
> **BOB BISHOP**

Previous spread: Cue Card (right)
jumps alongside Champion Court
before securing a second success
at the Cheltenham Festival in the
2013 Ryanair Chase

"He made my spine tingle the day he won the Champion Bumper and he's done it again today. Joe was so confident but my heart was pumping like hell. Our biggest worry was over whether to take on that big black horse. Thank God we didn't, but I wouldn't be surprised if we take him on again one day."

Cue Card's next days are expected to be at Aintree and Punchestown, where the targets will be obvious. The 33-year-old winning jockey, whose first festival win came on Earthmover 15 years ago, thought this one was as well.

"After watching Sprinter Sacre yesterday we knew we'd made the right decision," said Tizzard. "We could have run a gallant second to him but it's all about being first.

"I didn't really appreciate it when I was winning on Earthmover and then Flagship Uberalles. After that I went 11 years without a festival winner and now it's special.

"So much hard work goes into it and it's a big family thing. When it goes right it means a lot more, but when it goes wrong it hurts a lot more as well."

RACING POST ANALYSIS: It was run at a good gallop early, before slowing down, and a couple of the runners cracked under the pressure. The fact that Cue Card, who was the one dictating matters, pushed by Champion Court who finished very tired, was able to gallop on relentlessly for an authoritative success suggests this was the top-class performance it looked. Winner of the Champion Bumper in 2010, and a clear second to Sprinter Sacre in last season's Arkle, he's appeared an improved performer this season and, looking at how he saw this out, it's quite probable after all that he'd have beaten Captain Chris (blundered when challenging) at Ascot last time. Jumping well on the whole, he's a horse with an enormous amount of raw ability and the Melling Chase at Aintree next month looks tailor-made. As for next season, all options are open according to connections, who mentioned another crack at 3m as well as another possible shot at Sprinter Sacre being in their minds, so exciting times lie ahead for the seven-year-old.

> "
> He made my spine tingle the day he won the Champion Bumper and he's done it again today"
>
> **COLIN TIZZARD**

CHELTENHAM
Ryanair Chase

"With a horse like Sprinter Sacre, you'd be foolish not to take his plans into consideration. He's not like any other horse I know. He's the most brilliant horse I've seen. He looks as though he'd take the world of beating, but over two miles four around Aintree, you'd have to think it would play to all Cue Card's aces."

It did, in the sense Cue Card produced an even better performance at Aintree than he had at Cheltenham, improving his personal best Racing Post Rating from 176 to 178.

It did not, in the sense Sprinter Sacre ambled past Cue Card in between the final two fences with Barry Geraghty sitting motionless.

Following the race, Aintree racegoer Paddy Woods, the man who in the black and white era rode Arkle every morning, said of Sprinter Sacre: "He's definitely the best I've seen since Arkle. He has everything."

As such, it was no disgrace to again take silver behind a truly great gold medallist.

That was undoubtedly Joe Tizzard's take on the race.

"I'm as proud as hell of Cue Card," he said in the Aintree winner's enclosure. His father added: "Sprinter Sacre is the best I've seen and to me would stay any trip. I don't think I'd be in a hurry to take him on again. Once a year is enough!"

The two horses would never meet again. Both, however, would continue to write some wonderful stories.

> "
> Sprinter Sacre is the best I've seen and to me would stay any trip. I don't think I'd be in a hurry to take him on again. Once a year is enough!"
>
> **COLIN TIZZARD**

Joe Tizzard and Cue Card are in the lead but go on to finish second behind old adversary Sprinter Sacre in the Melling Chase at Aintree in April 2013

3
TOUGH GOING

Previous spread: Cue Card secures his first victory in the Betfair Chase at Haydock in November 2013 in the hands of regular jockey Joe Tizzard

IT WAS already impossible not to love Cue Card.

Here was a horse who relished his job and performed it to a wonderfully high level. He was a dual Cheltenham Festival winner at the age of seven, and although Sprinter Sacre had proved to be his master more than once, the display in defeat at Aintree was as good as anything Cue Card had achieved in victory.

As the new season started, there was talk from connections of trying to secure victory in the sport's ultimate prize, the Cheltenham Gold Cup. Before that the intention was to go back to the King George VI Chase via Haydock's hugely valuable Betfair Chase, a race Kauto Star had made his own by winning it four times.

First, though, Cue Card was sent back to Exeter for his reappearance outing. He had won the 2012 Haldon Gold Cup by a massive 26 lengths, but on that occasion he was racing off a BHA rating of 157. For the defence of his crown he was up to 172 and required to concede upwards of 17lb to every one of his five opponents, all of whom were talented chasers in their own right.

As such, it was no disgrace not to win, even allowing for the fact bookmakers returned him the 11-10 favourite. A slip at the fourth fence caused a predictable loss of confidence. The lead was lost but quickly regained, and although he was again headed at the third-last fence, he kept on with characteristic commitment to the cause and finished third, six and a quarter lengths behind the saluting Somersby. In terms of performance, he had still run to a figure at least a stone greater than any other horse in the Haldon field.

There was more than enough in his effort to suggest the team had every justification in continuing to aim high. At Haydock, they aimed very high indeed.

Cue Card had practically walked through the final strides of his first attempt at three miles. That said, it was easy to find plausible excuses for his tame finishing effort in the 2012 King George. It was equally easy to find reasons why the 2013 Betfair Chase might find him out in more ways than one.

For a start, there was the three-mile distance. Then there was the ground, which was soft and therefore likely to accentuate the race's stamina demands.

EXETER
BetVictor Haldon
Gold Cup Chase

2009-10					2010-11				2011-12				2012-13				2013-14			
JAN	FEB	MAR	APR	NOV	DEC	JAN	FEB	MAR	APR	NOV	DEC	JAN	FEB	MAR	APR	NOV	DEC	JAN	FEB	MAR	APR	NOV	DEC	JAN	FEB

The most daunting aspect of the Betfair Chase, however, was the opposition. The field included Gold Cup winner Bobs Worth, dual King George VI Chase hero Long Run and the 2012 Betfair Chase victor Silviniaco Conti. Add in one of the previous season's most exciting novices, Dynaste, and the latest staging of the Betfair Chase looked like being one to savour.

Assessing the mission, Colin Tizzard said: "The two-milers were pushing him a bit at Exeter and we haven't proved he's not a three-miler yet. There is a shortage of two-and-a-half-mile races so we want to have another look.

Cue Card (centre) was unable to repeat the previous year's victory in the Haldon Gold Cup at Exeter when third behind Somersby (right) and Module

3.00   **Betfair Chase (Registered As The**
[OFF 3.01]   **Lancashire Chase) Grade**
     1 Class 1   3m1f
Fav: 5-y-o and up **1st** £112,540 2nd £42,400 3rd £21,220 4th £10,600 5th £5,320 6th
£2,660

1   **CUE CARD** 7 11-7 ....(172) **Joe Tizzard**
     b g by King's Theatre (IRE)–Wicked Crack (IRE) (King's Ride)
     (Colin Tizzard) took keen hold early on, with leader, led 4th, made
     rest, ridden after last, stayed on to draw clear final 110yds
                                [tchd 10/1] **9/1**

2   4½ **DYNASTE (FR)** 7 11-7 ....(159) Tom Scudamore
     gr g by Martaline–Bellissima de Mai (FR) (Pistolet Bleu (IRE))
     (David Pipe) held up, headway 14th, tracked leaders 4 out, went
     2nd and challenged winner 2 out, ridden and not quicken run-in,
     one pace and held final 110yds [bets of £5500-£1000,
     £2750-£500]   [tchd 5/1] **11/2**

3   1¾ **SILVINIACO CONTI (FR)** 7 11-7 ....(173)   Noel Fehily
     [5¾] ch g by Dom Alco (FR)–Gazelle Lulu (FR) (Altayan)
     (Paul Nicholls) in touch, improved 10th, went 2nd after 11th, every
     chance 3 out, ridden and lost 2nd 2 out, not quicken before last,
     kept on under pressure towards finish [bet of £7000-£2000]
                         [tchd 10/3 and 4/1] **7/2**

"He wasn't stopping when he won over two-miles-four or two-miles-five last season and all his best work was after the last.

"It's a very hot race but he's had a run and I'm sure he'll run to his best."

He did, as David Carr made clear in his Haydock report.

If it's good enough for Desert Orchid, it's good enough for Cue Card. That's quite a comparison, but then he's quite a horse.

Just like Dessie, he is a chaser long seen as a two-miler, possibly effective at two and a half miles but too keen to last out a stayer's trip.

Desert Orchid famously proved that all wrong by running his rivals into the ground when stepped up to three miles in the King George VI Chase at Kempton in 1986 and Joe Tizzard had the guts to follow Simon Sherwood's bold tactical game plan 27 years on.

There was no hanging around at the back hoping to eke out his stamina.

Tizzard had the courage of his convictions, attacking from the front and taking up the running from as early as the fourth of the race's 18 fences.

Plenty of punters had doubted the three miles and one furlong of the best-ever Betfair Chase would prove within his compass and Cue Card started at 9-1 – but Desert Orchid went off at 16-1 on that memorable Boxing Day and Colin Tizzard's pride and joy, winner of the Champion Bumper and Ryanair Chase at past Cheltenham Festivals, proved similarly rewarding to those who kept faith in him.

The trainer's son and stable jockey was challenged in the home straight by first Noel Fehily, on last year's winner Silviniaco Conti, and then Tom Scudamore, on the up-and-coming Dynaste, but neither could get to the front.

Cue Card, who now trades between 5-1 and 8-1 for the Gold Cup, had seen them both off soon after the final fence and came home a four-and-a-half-length winner, with last season's Gold Cup hero Bobs Worth almost 40 lengths back in sixth.

HAYDOCK
Betfair Chase

The disappointing Cheltenham champion is as big as 6-1 with Ladbrokes to retain his prize in March.

Reflecting on his tactics, Joe Tizzard said: "I was very positive but he got into a rhythm like he did when he won the Ryanair, always saving a bit in front – he had his ears pricked and was loving it. I probably outstayed them in the end. They got to him and he's had to battle and has gone and done it well.

"That is the privilege of riding a faster horse, they are able to be going a gear less than the rest of them and it showed today."

Tizzard himself was the first to point out that waiting with him on his first crack over three miles at Kempton last year had been rather less of a success.

"In the King George we tried to hold on to him a little bit and he nearly fell at the first, missed the second and I was never comfortable on him," he said.

"The King George did him a world of good because it got him tired. Ever since then, once he gets in front he waits, he doesn't try to go as fast as he can for two miles. He's learned to race and that makes my life a lot easier.

"We were confident he was in good shape. He did a lovely piece of work on Sunday and schooled very well on Tuesday morning. Obviously he had hard questions to answer trip-wise, but we haven't got to worry about that now."

Colin Tizzard was convinced the tactics were right, and said: "Joe wasn't worried if someone wanted to take him on.

"If they go faster than him they're probably going too fast.

"After his first bumper he tried to bolt all the time and in the Champion Bumper he was a runaway horse, but he's easy to ride now.

"It would have been easier to stay at two miles because that's where his best form was and we were looking at the two-mile-three race at Ascot today, but this proves he does stay."

Cue Card had managed only third on his comeback under top weight in the Haldon Gold Cup, but the trainer was confident that outing had done wonders for the seven-year-old, along with a serious workout last weekend.

> **"**
> He had hard questions
> to answer trip-wise,
> but we haven't got to
> worry about that now"
> **JOE TIZZARD**

2014-15   2015-16   2016-17   2017-18

MAR | APR | NOV | DEC | JAN | FEB | MAR | APR | NOV | DEC | JAN | FEB | MAR | APR | NOV | DEC | JAN | FEB | MAR | APR | NOV | DEC | JAN | FEB | MAR | APR

> He's become a
> beautifully accurate
> jumper – he was
> like poetry today"

COLIN TIZZARD

Cue Card (right) and the rest of the
high-class field gather at the start before
the 2013 Betfair Chase at Haydock

"I gave him a good grilling last weekend," he said. "He was brilliant today, wasn't he? He jumped better than he ever has. He's become a beautifully accurate jumper – he was like poetry today. He was on his game for sure."

His son has long harboured hopes for Cue Card over a longer trip and said: "It is something we always hoped would happen – and now it's put some life in the Gold Cup."

But the father stressed: "There is plenty of water to go under the bridge yet. I'd assume if he is fine he will go for the King George."

Bookmakers reckon he is the one to beat in the Kempton race, for which he is 5-2 favourite with sponsors William Hill, while Gold Cup sponsors Betfred are among those quoting 8-1 for Cheltenham.

HAYDOCK
Betfair Chase

Cue Card (right) denies Dynaste (left)
and Silviniaco Conti in the Betfair Chase

Further success might mean more work at home in Bexhill for owner Jean Bishop, who joked: "We'll want new walls for the pictures – we will have to move or have an extension! I'm not grumbling, though.

"It looks as if the horse thoroughly enjoyed himself and I hope all the people who have always doubted him look at that and eat their words."

RACING POST RATINGS: Cue Card started the race a doubtful stayer, but after negotiating 3m1f and 18 fences in soft ground around Haydock, he stayed on better than anything else to land a superb renewal of the Betfair Chase.

It was a stellar front-running performance from Colin Tizzard's star, who saw off Grade 1 winner after Grade 1 winner to maintain his lead before pinging the last to come home four and a half lengths clear of last season's leading three-mile novice Dynaste.

The field was one of the strongest assembled for the Haydock feature and after a decisive win, Cue Card ranks among the jumping world's finest on an RPR of 180.

He also takes high rank against past winners of the race, sitting joint-second on the list of Betfair Chase heroes – a list previously dominated by Kauto Star.

BETFAIR CHASE WINNERS How they rated	
Winner	RPR
Kauto Star (2006)	184
Cue Card (2013)	180
Kauto Star (2007)	180
Kauto Star (2011)	177
Kauto Star (2009)	177
Silviniaco Conti (2012)	173
Imperial Commander (2010)	172
Kingscliff (2005)	168
Snoopy Loopy (2008)	167

Cue Card with Joe Tizzard and his delighted owners Jean and Bob Bishop

We'll want new walls for the pictures – we will have to move or have an extension!"

JEAN BISHOP

The result was a defining moment for Cue Card. After dispelling the 2m4f myth with a career-best show over the longest distance he had encountered, the Cheltenham Gold Cup must loom large on his agenda.

Although it feels as if he's been around forever, he's only seven and after showing gradual but consistent progress over the last few seasons, there is a chance there could be more to come.

After 12 chases he has just the right balance of youth and experience and, given his excellent record at the Cheltenham Festival, he has to rate a serious contender for the Gold Cup in March.

As a confirmed Cue Card fan, Alastair Down had no words to eat – but you sense he enjoyed writing these words.

HAYDOCK
Betfair Chase

2009-10				2010-11					2011-12					2012-13					2013-14			
JAN	FEB	MAR	APR	NOV	DEC	JAN	FEB	MAR	APR	NOV	DEC	JAN	FEB	MAR	APR	NOV	DEC	JAN	FEB	MAR	APR	NOV	DEC	JAN	FEB

An emotional Colin Tizzard is interviewed after Cue Card's victory in the Betfair Chase

Although only seven, there was an element of Cue Card coming of age yesterday when, in a display of almost contagious enthusiasm, he surpassed his already considerable achievements by bossing a gold-standard Betfair Chase field into a state of total submission.

Leading at the fourth, Joe Tizzard got a terrific tune out of Cue Card, who put his heart into each and every one of Haydock's beefed-up fences and, seeming to relish every minute, saw it out up the straight like a Trojan as his two closest pursuers struggled to no avail in their efforts to lay a glove on him.

Indeed, from the fourth-last it was a case of the West's awake as the pride of Dorset pinged away in the lead with the West Country pair of Silviniaco Conti and Dynaste still looking potent threats with the rest toiling back in the boondocks.

But this cracking chaser, who has mixed it at the highest level almost since day one and scrapped his way up the ranks from pulverising Champion Bumper winner, through Ryanair triumph to this – his finest hour – was not for catching.

He has always been campaigned fearlessly and the Tizzards and his owners the Bishops have never ducked a confrontation with him for the simple reason their belief in him has never wavered. Cue Card would have turned up at the OK Corral if Colin Tizzard had remembered to put him in at the five-day stage.

> **"**
> He surpassed his already considerable achievements by bossing a gold-standard Betfair Chase field into a state of total submission"
>
> **ALASTAIR DOWN**

2014-15　2015-16　2016-17　2017-18

MAR | APR | NOV | DEC | JAN | FEB | MAR | APR | NOV | DEC | JAN | FEB | MAR | APR | NOV | DEC | JAN | FEB | MAR | APR | NOV | DEC | JAN | FEB | MAR | APR

> **"**
> He got into a
> lovely rhythm,
> had his ears pricked
> and was loving it"
>
> **JOE TIZZARD**

And just think of the heat of the races he has not won – he was sent off 7-4 favourite for the 2011 Supreme Novices' Hurdle when two of the three who beat him were Al Ferof and Sprinter Sacre. And in the last two seasons he had two brave cracks at Sprinter Sacre, which is the sort of hard-labour diet that might lead a less ferociously competitive horse to have second thoughts about giving your all only to get a pasting.

But Cue Card still relishes it and as Joe Tizzard said: "He got into a lovely rhythm, had his ears pricked and was loving it. He outstayed them in the end and that's the best he's ever been."

If Colin Tizzard embarrassed himself by shedding a tear, he didn't embarrass anyone else.

There are people who dissolve into the salty stuff when their little darling appears as eighth shepherd in the nativity play and, while the last time the trainer wept was when hearing the price his wholesaler was offering for the milk from his cows, there would have been something wrong with him if he hadn't found a tear on this occasion – his own son triumphing in a great race on the horse of both their lifetimes.

And for good reason Cue Card is one of those horses the public have taken to their hearts.

It's partly the Tizzard father-and-son element and also the fact his owners, Bob and Jean Bishop, don't have dozens in training and a cheque book that is so busy it never cools to room temperature. But it's mainly the horse himself – jumping people love a trier and he is never less than that.

Nor is he wrapped in cotton wool. Tizzard senior came out with a marvellously descriptive line when, having reflected that Cue Card had come on a lot for his seasonal pipe-opener at Exeter, he said: "I gave him a good grilling last weekend just to make sure."

This was the day when the two and two-and-a-half-mile speedster stepped up another level and, more importantly, annexed different territory – that of the staying chaser. He will go to Kempton for the King George to put right last year's wrong when he ran one of his very few poor races.

HAYDOCK
Betfair Chase

Will we see him at Cheltenham on Festival Friday? Well, Colin Tizzard described the Gold Cup as "everybody's dream" – and that is the truth.

Having never ducked a fight with Cue Card you can hardly see any Bishop or Tizzard turning down the chance of realising that dream.

Festival Friday was clearly on their minds. Speaking a few days after the brilliance of the Betfair Chase, Colin Tizzard confirmed a tilt at the Gold Cup was more tempting than a Ryanair return ticket.

"I've got the owner sat beside me and he's nodding," said Tizzard. "It's got to be on the radar. It's everyone's dream to have a runner in the Gold Cup. There is no reason why we shouldn't, none at all. He likes Cheltenham – it is one of his best tracks so we'll look forward to it."

First, though, they were looking forward to the King George, for which Cue Card was heading the ante-post market, even allowing for the fact that as Christmas closed in there was a degree of concern for the health of the stable.

"We've had a bug, there's no two ways about it," said Tizzard senior. "I don't want to make out it's a big issue, but it is an issue.

"Quite a few of the lesser horses haven't been running up to scratch and some of them have been atrocious. They all look lovely until you run them but then they don't run so well.

"Cue Card might have had it in the Haldon as he didn't run quite so well that day. It's not like a cold because there's nothing visible. It makes the muscles twist and then when they run they tweak something.

"I thought Cue Card jumped a bit tight at Exeter whereas he was the most beautiful, fluent horse at Haydock. We don't want him coughing on Christmas Day and although we can't stop it we'll take every precaution."

Cue Card and the people surrounding him were hot property as the King George approached. Everyone wanted a piece of them, including the Racing Post's Peter Thomas, who headed to Dorset for some Tizzard time.

"

I thought Cue Card jumped a bit tight at Exeter whereas he was the most beautiful, fluent horse at Haydock"

COLIN TIZZARD

2014-15 2015-16 2016-17 2017-18

MAR | APR | NOV | DEC | JAN | FEB | MAR | APR | NOV | DEC | JAN | FEB | MAR | APR | NOV | DEC | JAN | FEB | MAR | APR | NOV | DEC | JAN | FEB | MAR | APR

There's a heady whiff in the little barn next to Colin and Pauline Tizzard's house, and it's not all down to the early morning huddle of Her Majesty's press corps at Venn Farm. Six pheasants are hanging from the rafters at roughly nose level and, to be frank, they look a lot better than they smell, so it's a relief when a phalanx of muddy 4x4s arrives to whisk us into the fresh air at the top of Colin's gallops.

Not surprisingly, with so many hacks involved, there's a lot of aimless shambling going on at the edge of the all-weather before the trainer suggests, with as much politeness as he can muster that, since "it's Monday morning and these horses won't be pissing about", we should possibly relocate to a safer vantage point.

In the middle of the circular sand canter, out of harm's way, we shuffle around in the damp Dorset air, unearthing turnips with our boots as we go, thinking perhaps that, if we could find a carrot field and an Oxo cube, we'd have not so much a high-end National Hunt training yard as the makings of a passable game stew.

That's the down-to-earth reality of life in the yard that houses Cue Card. The Tizzards may be in charge of the favourite for the King George VI Chase, but in this corner of the West Country they call a swede a swede. On Boxing Day they'll seek to climb one of the loftiest peaks in jump racing, but there will still be 250 cows to milk the next morning, win or lose.

And if they win, don't run away with the idea that the team will celebrate with a champagne reception and an open-top bus ride through the streets of Milborne Port. It's part superstition and possibly part frugality, but Yorkshire-born owner Bob Bishop, who along with his wife Jean paid €52,000 for the three-year-old at Fairyhouse four years ago, has become accustomed to a modest routine in the event of extraordinary success.

"After he won the Champion Bumper we had a sandwich in a Tesco's car park," he recalls. "When we won the Ryanair we went to a Burger King and on the way back from Haydock after the Betfair Chase last month, Jean, Colin, Pauline and

A magnificent-looking Cue Card at home with Colin Tizzard

I stopped for fish and chips at Yeovil. We know how to celebrate, that's for sure.

"I don't suppose the fish and chip shops will be open on Boxing Day, but we'll find somewhere if we need to."

The breakfast of champions this may not be, but there's no doubting the unadorned passion with which Colin, his jockey/son Joe and assistant/daughter Kim approach the challenge of their 70 horses in general and that of four-time Grade 1 winner Cue Card in particular. He's a horse who has frustrated, delighted, united and divided those who have followed his career, yet after splitting opinion for four years, the speedy, 'non-staying' son of King's Theatre finds himself on the brink of being regarded as the best staying chaser in Britain and a robust contender for next year's Cheltenham Gold Cup.

Even Tizzard senior and Bishop confess to having doubted they had a long-distance runner on their hands, but Joe, with the certainty of youth, seems never to have wavered in his belief. Perhaps it's simply the confidence of a man who once caught his head in a hay-baler and lived to tell the tale, but Tizzard junior's uncomplicated faith in the horse comes as something of a tonic after several seasons of multi-faceted doubt.

This may be a horse with speed to burn, seems to be the message, but all his life has been a prelude to a career as a staying chaser, as evidenced by a personal-best effort over three miles and a furlong at Haydock last time, when he left two Gold Cup winners trailing in his substantial wake. Now comes the chance to set the record straight after a flop in last year's King George that stoked the embers of the stamina debate.

"Last year's Kempton run played on my mind at Haydock," says Joe, "but we said we'd just let him go and do it. He's bred to get the trip – his mother Wicked Crack wanted four and a half miles, she was slow – and we've always thought he would.

"In fact, I really believe the King George made him as a racehorse. He made a couple of mistakes and got very tired, which had never happened to him before, and after that he

"
I really believe the King George made him as a racehorse"

JOE TIZZARD

doesn't pull any more. Horses do learn but sometimes it takes a really hard race to make them think they need to save a bit for the end.

"Now, if someone wants to go quicker than his comfort zone, they're probably going too quick. That's the advantage of having the fastest horse in a three-mile race – I can wait until the last and if anybody wants to sprint from there, there's no doubt he's quicker than them."

It's a view the owner will be happy to take as gospel. Tizzard has been riding for the Bishops for ten years now and has been on board Cue Card for all 19 of his runs, from the debut success in a Fontwell bumper to this season's disappointing failure to hang on to his Haldon Gold Cup crown and his subsequent redemption at Haydock.

But Bishop goes back a lot further than his association with Venn Farm. He part-owned his first horse, the Fulke Walwyn-trained Men Of Yorkshire, no less than 28 years ago, when he was deputy chairman of Crystal Palace FC in the days of Malcolm Allison and Terry Venables, and the 80-year-old, who sold his insurance loss-adjusting investigation business in 1986, has been a man of the turf ever since.

While it has been a long haul for the owner, however, life with the Tizzards has given him not only his best horse by some margin but also the pleasure of seeing the unvarnished pleasure of the sport at first hand. Here, among the pheasants and the turnips, he has found the roots of National Hunt, with hunting people who hark back to the era of racing as a part of country life.

If Colin Tizzard were ever to appear on *What's My Line?*, it would take no more than three seconds for the panel to guess he was a farmer. The stout, ruddy-cheeked yeoman was born in a caravan in Milborne Port, the village where his father Les started out living in the Queen's Head, keeping a handful of cows in what became the skittle alley.

Venn Farm grew up around the young family, but while the keen junior cricketer and his two brothers all went on to farm

"

When Dad retires
I'll take over the farm
and the training"

JOE TIZZARD

the surrounding acres, it was Colin who channelled more and more of his efforts into point-to-pointing, bringing the operation to a sharper focus when Joe began to ride, then setting to work building a licensed jumps yard that thrived for the hill up which his horses work and on which his father is now buried.

Joe blossomed and went off to seek his fortune as first jockey to Paul Nicholls – a job that went famously pear-shaped for the callow youth – but now he's back, working almost as hard as Dad and surprising himself with the way in which he has embraced farming as part of his identity.

"If you'd asked me ten years ago I wouldn't have said it, but now I enjoy the farm," he says. "I run it and it's an important part of the business, and a massive part of my life. If we're not racing we're at home on the farm, and with not much racing this week and all this rain, we'll start getting the young stock in from the fields.

"I suppose you could call it a diversion, but I'm not the kind to wind myself up about a big race anyway. I'll sleep well on Christmas night – it's just how I am. I'm lucky like that."

While Joe has no worries about the big day, neither Colin nor Bob has any worry about Joe, either, although Colin worries about some of the things his boy likes to jump when he's out hunting and isn't quite ready to surrender control of the business to such a reckless youth.

"He'll bloody kill himself one of these days," he frowns, with the look of a man who'd like still to be jumping the same obstacles himself. "He's a damn good chase jockey but there's a bigger picture now.

"He's 34 and he doesn't do less than 10st 10lb any more, but most of our owners still want him and he's the one I rely on to tell me what I need to know in the morning.

"But I'm the one who's training them still. I manage the horses and he manages the farm and I don't know if I'm ready to move over yet."

Joe, of course, takes a rather more dramatic view of the future. "When Dad retires I'll take over the farm and the training," he grins. "I think we could milk 500 cows and train 200 racehorses – and have a thousand acres of arable. It's easy, isn't it, just crack on and keep ourselves busy."

While the exact course of the succession is being decided, Brendan Powell is being groomed as number one jockey of the future, although at the moment his progress is being hindered by a Vauxhall Zafira that's blocked him in on the driveway. A call to Colin on the gallops quickly ascertains that the culprit, unsurprisingly, is a gormless hack who is dispatched to move the offending vehicle and allow Powell to fulfil his destiny in the first at Plumpton.

The abuse is short-lived and good-natured, however, as befits a welcoming household that until recently boasted Pauline's bed-and-breakfast as part of its economic plan. "She doesn't really do it any more," says Colin. "I supply her with too much money these days!"

Colin Tizzard pictured at Venn Farm stables at the end of 2014

The Bishops have certainly fallen for the charms of Venn Farm and Bob is happy to leave the horse in safe hands over Christmas while he enjoys the festive season with his clan down on the East Sussex coast, managing another half who's rather less relaxed about the big race.

The only doubt in his mind surrounds a low-grade bug that seems to have been stalking the yard all season, but that problem he'll consign to the tray marked 'not much we can do about it'.

"We've got a very close family and eight or ten of us will be together for Christmas lunch and going to Kempton together on Boxing Day," Bishop says. "There's bound to be a bit of tension and I've got a wife who is a very, very quiet lady but won't sleep for the last two or three nights before the race.

"She'll be fine on the day and she's greatly looking forward to it, but it wouldn't be natural if you didn't get nervous, would it?

"I'm the greatest pessimist in the world and I never count my chickens, which was why I rang Colin at quarter past five on the morning of the Haydock race, worried not so much about the trip but about the bug in the yard.

"The way he ran at Exeter the time before, even in the parade ring, it was obvious he wasn't himself and I wondered about taking him all the way to Haydock and asking him to run three miles and a furlong for the first time in the best company of the season.

"But Colin was so confident that we agreed to run, and we got it right, didn't we?

"I think if he turns up in the same form as that, it'll take a very good horse to beat him, and we know that if the bug affects him at Kempton, Joe will always take care of him."

Colin, meanwhile, takes the attention in his stride, hoping like Bishop that Cue Card may have shrugged off the dreaded bug in time to deliver the defining performance of his career. Doubts about the horse's powers of endurance have now been banished and the trainer already has one eye focused on the middle distance, beyond December and on into March.

" I'm the greatest pessimist in the world and I never count my chickens, which was why I rang Colin at quarter past five on the morning of the Haydock race, worried not so much about the trip but about the bug in the yard"

BOB BISHOP

"We'll see after Boxing Day, but it wouldn't be our way to go for the Ryanair," he says. "Everyone wants a runner in the Gold Cup and I'll never have a better chance.

"I don't think he'll be beaten for stamina – it might even be that he wants three and a quarter miles at Cheltenham, the way most bumper horses do – and although good horses have beaten Cue Card before, the ones in behind him at Haydock probably had a harder race than he did and we're probably the one to beat.

"Do I feel the pressure? I get the flu once a fortnight now – it comes with the responsibility. I don't want him to go there needing a run and you can't pussyfoot around with his work, but that comes with risks attached and it's a fine line to tread."

I think half of Dorset was crying with me"
COLIN TIZZARD

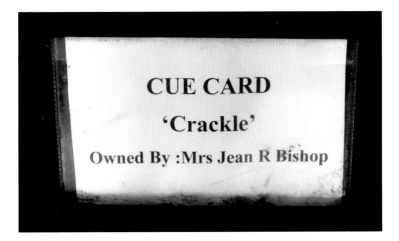

Cue Card's name card on his box at Venn Farm stables

The only question remaining concerns the post-race scenes if Cue Card should deliver at Kempton. Will Colin collapse in the same blubbing heap he became at Haydock – "I think half of Dorset was crying with me," he says, by way of mitigation – or will he have become so accustomed to big-race victory that he'll retain a stony-faced silence?

Joe has his opinion on the matter: "It was fantastic round the kitchen table the next morning. The women stick up for him and say it was lovely to see, but the men have pulled his leg a bit and I had my half-hour of pure bliss."

Bob Bishop, though, is rather more forgiving: "I don't mind if he cries his bloody eyes out for a week if we win. There's no shame in a good weep at the right time."

It turned out that tears, had they been seen to fall following the 2013 King George, would have been understandable, albeit for all the wrong reasons.

In the Racing Post's King George preview, Colin Tizzard spoke in bullish terms, observing: "Everything is right for him. I don't think I've ever seen him so well."

The trainer also made clear Cue Card would be ridden from the front, as he had been so successfully at Haydock. For most of the Kempton classic he was indeed in front – and for most of it he looked like staying in front. Quite why he did not will remain one of those forever unanswered questions.

He would subsequently undergo a wind operation, suggesting a breathing problem might have been a factor, but the simple fact of the matter is Cue Card went from being a seemingly certain winner to an unlikely loser in a matter of strides.

Having set a strong pace from flag fall, he was still travelling powerfully entering the home straight, with nearest rival Silviniaco Conti two to three lengths behind and toiling. The deficit remained unchanged as Cue Card landed over the penultimate fence.

Then something happened. Perhaps when Joe Tizzard looked over his left shoulder he knew there was a major problem. It was as though the thoroughbred beneath him was a car that had suddenly run out of petrol. At the furlong pole Cue Card was passed. At the final fence he was already a length and a half behind an opponent he knew so well. Through the closing stages he saw only the back of him.

As shocked as everyone else, I wrote this in the minutes that followed the race Cue Card seemed destined to win but then lost.

Jumping the second-last fence he seemed certain to win but by the time the final fence was reached he was booked for second.

KEMPTON
William Hill King
George VI Chase

2009-10   2010-11   2011-12   2012-13   **2013-14**

JAN | FEB | MAR | APR | NOV | DEC | JAN | FEB | MAR | APR | NOV | DEC | JAN | FEB | MAR | APR | NOV | DEC | JAN | FEB | MAR | APR | NOV | DEC | JAN | FEB

Cue Card finishes runner-up to Silviniaco Conti in his second King George at Kempton

The scales tipped quickly for Cue Card, but although the fuel gauge ran out, connections went home delighted with the 100-30 joint-favourite and far from ruling out a tilt at the Betfred Cheltenham Gold Cup.

As expected, Joe Tizzard set out to make all and the tactics looked set to be successfully executed until his mount weakened rapidly in between the final two fences.

Even so, there were still 11 lengths back to Al Ferof in third, and with many reckoning Cue Card to be better left-handed,

2014-15   2015-16   2016-17   2017-18

MAR | APR | NOV | DEC | JAN | FEB | MAR | APR | NOV | DEC | JAN | FEB | MAR | APR | NOV | DEC | JAN | FEB | MAR | APR | NOV | DEC | JAN | FEB | MAR | APR

and perhaps also on quicker ground, it remains likely Tizzard's father Colin and owners Bob and Jean Bishop will aim for the Gold Cup in preference to a repeat Ryanair Chase bid. The Gold Cup sponsors quote him at 8-1.

"He just got outstayed in the end but was brilliant again," said Colin Tizzard. "The rest were miles back. I would think it will be the Gold Cup for us but the Ryanair is tempting."

Joe Tizzard was equally pleased with Cue Card. "I'm not disappointed," he said. "He has run his heart out and right on a par with Haydock.

"I tried to fill him up going round the bend but in the end the winner just outstayed me. We'll take him on again on better ground. I think if we get good or good to soft ground at Cheltenham we'll probably end up in the Gold Cup, but there's a lot to discuss between now and then."

Their positivity was not rewarded with compensation, not for some time at least.

No sooner had the owners and trainer confirmed Cue Card would run in the Gold Cup, as opposed to the Ryanair Chase, it was announced in late February he would be running nowhere for the rest of the season.

Bob Bishop, the enthusiastic owner of dual Cheltenham Festival winner Cue Card, was left devastated yesterday by the news his pride and joy would miss out on jump racing's Olympics.

Cue Card had been an 8-1 chance for the Gold Cup and 4-1 favourite with some firms for the Ryanair, before Tizzard told the Racing Post he would not make either race, the revelation coming two days after Sprinter Sacre's defection from the Champion Chase.

"According to Colin, Cue Card looked a million dollars this morning, so he decided to take him and Theatre Guide, who has also had a bit of a setback, up the gallop," said Bishop, who shares ownership of his horses with wife Jean.

> **"**
> He just got outstayed in the end but was brilliant again"
> **COLIN TIZZARD**

KEMPTON
William Hill King
George VI Chase

"But he rang about 20 minutes later and said both horses have got to come out. They got to the top of the gallop and were both slightly lame. I'm devastated."

Tizzard explained: "He's not been quite right behind for a week and we've done everything we possibly can to try to rectify the problem, but the decision has been made with the owners this morning not to run at Cheltenham. It appears he has pulled muscles in his back."

Bob Bishop with his wife Jean, groom Catrin Eynon and Cue Card after their star chaser's victory at Cheltenham in November 2010

Cue Card would not race again that season. He would never race again under Joe Tizzard. The pair had taken part in 20 races together, winning ten of them.

Here's how I responded to Joe's decision to stop being a jockey in a Racing Post tribute.

When Joe Tizzard told mother Pauline on Friday of his decision to retire with immediate effect she burst into tears. She was delighted. So should we all be.

There was, of course, a degree of slightly selfish sadness on learning a jockey who has been part of our racing lives for 17 years will no longer be seen in silks and breeches. That is inev-

2014-15   2015-16   2016-17   2017-18

MAR | APR | NOV | DEC | JAN | FEB | MAR | APR | NOV | DEC | JAN | FEB | MAR | APR | NOV | DEC | JAN | FEB | MAR | APR | NOV | DEC | JAN | FEB | MAR | APR

itable and is bound to form a degree of our response. Mostly, however, we should applaud and celebrate whenever a jump jockey of such long standing gets out of the sport at a time of his or her own choosing, with body, brain and future all intact. That is the sort of retirement we should want for all those who participate in what Channel 4 reminded us with its latest Grand National trailer is the original extreme sport.

When speaking about his decision to quit, Tizzard said he had been thinking about it for 24 hours. For most major life decisions that would seem an extraordinarily short space of time in which to consider a drastic reshaping of a life. Not so for jump jockeys. Theirs is an existence in constant pursuit of an adrenaline rush so few of us will ever experience. Once the almost obsessive desire to embrace that feeling fades, it is time to raise the shutters. Better to stop a year too soon than to continue for a day too long. Tizzard has undoubtedly made the right call.

Yet the words of praise coming from his weighing room colleagues highlight how much he will be missed. Jockeys are a close-knit bunch, connected by a camaraderie that is both special and rare. Not everyone, however, can be loved. Not every guy can be a good guy. While some will be treasured, others will be tolerated.

Tizzard was evidently treasured, as anyone who follows racing's leading riders on social media will have seen very clearly over the last few days. One generally does not speak ill of the dead, nor indeed retiring jump jockeys, but one also seldom hears so much enthusiastic praise and heartfelt tributes being expressed towards a member of the band.

Not even Tizzard's closest friends or most dedicated admirers would say he was a great jockey, but exceptionally few jockeys merit that description. Tizzard was a very good jockey, almost certainly as time went on a significantly underrated jockey, and one whose achievements should not be overlooked.

His was a career of two halves, one linked to Paul Nicholls, the other linked to his father.

Opposite: Joe Tizzard enjoys one of his finest moments on Cue Card in the Ryanair Chase at Cheltenham in 2013

2009-10 2010-11 2011-12 2012-13 2013-14
JAN | FEB | MAR | APR | NOV | DEC | JAN | FEB | MAR | APR | NOV | DEC | JAN | FEB | MAR | APR | NOV | DEC | JAN | FEB | MAR | APR | NOV | DEC | JAN | FEB

2014–15 2015–16 2016–17 2017–18

MAR | APR | NOV | DEC | JAN | FEB | MAR | APR | NOV | DEC | JAN | FEB | MAR | APR | NOV | DEC | JAN | FEB | MAR | APR | NOV | DEC | JAN | FEB | MAR | APR

Daryl Jacob, who showed his own class with a beautiful letter in yesterday's Racing Post, has discovered this season that riding for a top stable is not always easy, in the main because a powerful operation will have powerful owners, some of whom are keen to wield their power. The opinions of some owners in any major yard can be hard to understand and their views might be based more around ignorance and egotism, but the bill-payers ensure equine stars can play for the team and their desires must therefore be satisfied. When stable jockey at Ditcheat, Tizzard learned that to his cost.

To his credit, particularly given how young he was at the time, he took any reverses or dents to his pride quietly and with dignity. For a while, Nicholls used him when he could and, speaking over the weekend, he described seeing his former number one win the Ryanair Chase on Cue Card as one of his personal racing highlights.

That victory provided one of the most memorable moments of Tizzard's second coming as a jockey, the alliance with his father Colin providing both men with the opportunity to shine on the sport's biggest stages.

Yet even when working for the family, Tizzard was reminded that some owners will always want to make their voice heard by interfering in riding arrangements. Once again Tizzard first saw the bigger picture and then saw good sense. By not complaining, but instead nurturing the man those owners wanted – the much younger and more fashionable Brendan Powell – the yard's old stable jockey and his likely successor will hopefully both reap benefit.

Some jockeys, like entertainers, haircuts and tight trousers, go in and out of fashion. At times, not least when he became a record-breaking conditional champion with 91 winners in a season, Tizzard was in fashion. There were longer periods when he was not. It's easy to think of other once high-profile jockeys who now struggle to not just ride winners but to get rides. In the case of some, the fault is at least in part their own, but not for all. Those in that situation are hoping for a Cue

Card to come along. For Tizzard, many years after Flagship Uberalles and See More Business, one did.

That was sweet but sweeter still is he got out in one piece, when and how he wanted. Any jump jockey would surely settle for that.

Nobody else had ever ridden Cue Card in a race. It was revealed in June 2014 that Daryl Jacob would be the next man to do so after he was appointed first-choice jockey to Bob and Jean Bishop.

Cue Card shows his customary enthusiasm before finishing fourth in the 2014 Betfair Chase at Haydock

2014-15   2015-16   2016-17   2017-18
MAR APR NOV DEC JAN FEB MAR APR NOV DEC JAN FEB MAR APR NOV DEC JAN FEB MAR APR NOV DEC JAN FEB MAR APR

By the time of Jacob's first outing on Cue Card in the 2014 Haldon Gold Cup, the horse had, on top of recovering from the stress fracture that caused him to be sidelined, undergone a wind operation and had his palate cauterised.

Explaining why, Tizzard said: "We just thought in the King George he had the race won three out, then going to the second-last he stopped and we were just worried if his palate had come up. We checked it and it needed tweaking. It was nothing major."

What had been major was the length of time Tizzard had gone without a winner – 200 days – until Native River scored at Stratford on October 30.

Tizzard was by now once again in winning form. It would be some time before the same was true of Cue Card.

Back down in trip, there was nothing much wrong with his fourth under top weight at Exeter. He then filled the same position behind Silviniaco Conti in the Betfair Chase at Haydock, where Colin Tizzard reported his star athlete had given a good blow. He predicted improvement over the months ahead.

It did not materialise. At Kempton he could manage only fifth to Silviniaco Conti – him again – in the King George, following which a racecourse vet reported he had been struck into just under a fetlock. It was a significant cut that needed stitches. The Tizzard stable announced their flagbearer would not be able to run until Cheltenham.

It was then announced in early March he would not even run at Cheltenham.

"He's got a small wind problem that will be sorted today and he should be all right for Aintree," said Tizzard. "He's having the wind op today – a little correction – and everybody says he'll be fine in a week, but he won't be going to Cheltenham. He's started making a little noise in the last few days."

All was well come Aintree, but although Cue Card finished second to the following year's Gold Cup hero Don Cossack, a yawning gap of 26 lengths separated them. At Punchestown the honours again went to Don Cossack, as Cue Card, this time partnered by Aidan Coleman, finished fourth in the feature race of the track's festival.

"

He's got a small wind problem that will be sorted today and he should be all right for Aintree"

COLIN TIZZARD

"He had half a chance turning in and Aidan thought he stayed quite well," said Tizzard. "That opens up options like the Charlie Hall. I'm chuffed and now we just need to find a race he can win."

He would find more than one such race. Cue Card's story was not over. Nor was his rivalry with Don Cossack.

Cue Card (right) jumps alongside Don Cossack before finishing second in the Melling Chase at Aintree in April 2015

EXETER
Vix Technology Haldon
Gold Cup Chase

HAYDOCK
Betfair Chase

KEMPTON
William Hill
King George
VI Chase

AINTREE
Betfred Melling Chase

PUNCHESTOWN
Bibby Financial Services Ireland
Punchestown Gold Cup

	2014–15					2015–16					2016–17					2017–18			
MAR	APR	NOV	DEC	JAN	FEB	MAR	APR	NOV	DEC	JAN	FEB	MAR	APR	NOV	DEC	JAN	FEB	MAR	APR

4
KEMPTON
CHEER

Previous spread: Cue Card and Paddy Brennan (right) get the better of Vautour and Ruby Walsh in the 2015 King George VI Chase at Kempton

THERE WAS by now much for him to prove.

At the start of the 2015–16 season, Cue Card had been beaten in his last six races, dating back to the agony-inducing 2013 King George he seemed sure to win but then lost. On that afternoon he held an official rating of 174. By the time he returned his mark had plummeted to 160. He appeared to be a fading force.

Yet those closest to him had lost no faith, mainly because they believed an excuse had been found to explain the regression.

Speaking during the campaign's early autumn countdown, Colin Tizzard – who during the summer had relocated his training yard to a mile away from its predecessor – said: "We had a difficult time last season but he had a trapped epiglottis, a rare type of problem in which the skin comes up over the air pipe. It could have been what made him stop so quickly in the King George the year before last. He looked to have the race won that day."

Tizzard was also asked about a new bonus introduced by Jockey Club Racecourses, which had announced £1 million would be split between the owner, trainer, jockey and yard of a horse who managed to annexe the Betfair Chase, King George and Gold Cup.

"It looks nigh-on impossible to win all three," he said, adding: "That's why there's so much money up for grabs."

This was not to be the only time Tizzard would be asked the £1m question, but before further probing was necessary, Cue Card had to answer a question of his own. He needed to show he could still be a force. Under Paddy Brennan, the rider chosen to take over on his back, he did just that when reappearing in Wetherby's Charlie Hall Chase.

Tom O'Ryan was there to see him do it.

Don't say he didn't tell you.

"He's had the perfect preparation – there will be no excuses," said Colin Tizzard in yesterday's Racing Post about Cue Card's bid to return to the big time in the Charlie Hall Chase.

No excuses were needed as the nine-year-old, without a win since his memorable Betfair Chase victory nearly two years ago, bagged this Grade 2 showpiece in the hands of Paddy Brennan.

2009-10   2010-11   2011-12   2012-13   2013-14

JAN | FEB | MAR | APR | NOV | DEC | JAN | FEB | MAR | APR | NOV | DEC | JAN | FEB | MAR | APR | NOV | DEC | JAN | FEB | MAR | APR | NOV | DEC | JAN | FEB

Winner of more than £750,000 in prize-money for owners Jean and Bob Bishop, Cue Card prevailed by three and three-quarter lengths from Dynaste.

Tizzard was understandably thrilled. Having seen his long-time stable star reach a speed of 40mph when enjoying a race-course gallop at Wincanton last Monday, he took particular satisfaction in a job well done.

"After last year when he was troubled by a trapped epiglottis, which was so bad he could hardly trot up our gallop without gurgling, it's wonderful to see him back to something like his best," said Tizzard. "We brought him in a month early this time and he's been brilliant all the way through.

> It's wonderful to see him back to something like his best"

COLIN TIZZARD

Cue Card and Paddy Brennan get off to a perfect start in the Charlie Hall Chase at Wetherby in October 2015

WETHERBY
bet365 Charlie Hall Chase

2014–15   2015–16   2016–17   2017–18

MAR | APR | NOV | DEC | JAN | FEB | MAR | APR | NOV | DEC | JAN | FEB | MAR | APR | NOV | DEC | JAN | FEB | MAR | APR | NOV | DEC | JAN | FEB | MAR | APR

Paddy Brennan can't hide his delight after winning the Charlie Hall Chase on his first ride on Cue Card

" He jumped, he travelled, he settled – he was trained to the minute and my job was easy"

PADDY BRENNAN

"We'd had two or three horses blow up first time out this season, which was the reason I gave him a two-mile gallop around Wincanton. We couldn't risk bringing him here unless we were convinced he was fit. It probably stood him in good stead."

Tizzard was full of praise for the ride by Brennan – "Paddy's a confident man and he's been confident about this horse since the first time he schooled him" – and the jockey took great pleasure in adding a second Charlie Hall to his CV after securing first prize eight years ago aboard Ollie Magern.

"That was special, but this feels even better," said Brennan. "As you get older, it gets harder. This is a proud day for me. It's lovely to get on a horse of his calibre again. He jumped, he travelled, he settled – he was trained to the minute and my job was easy."

Plainly, after yesterday, Cue Card is a horse to take seriously again. But then Colin Tizzard knew that all along.

RACING POST ANALYSIS: Cue Card reportedly encouraged his connections in his preparations ahead of this first start in six months, having had problems with a trapped epiglottis last term. He usually goes well fresh at this time of year, and looked in good nick beforehand. He raced a tad freely, but jumped and travelled into a good lead from approaching four out, and bravely found more when appearing slightly vulnerable to the challenge of the two Pipe horses, who were also racing unpenalised here, before the last. It remains to be seen if he can build further on this popular winning return but better ground would certainly help on that score.

The northern tour continued the following month. At Haydock, Cue Card did not simply do what he did at Wetherby. He did it to a completely different level.

The 2015 Betfair Chase attracted just five runners, but one of them was Silviniaco Conti, seeking to extend his own fabulous big-race haul with a third success in Haydock's annual showpiece.

He ran a good race, but on this occasion Cue Card was exceptional, as David Carr's report makes clear.

There's a new *Dad's Army* film coming out early next year but if you want to see much-loved characters making an unexpected and highly popular comeback, head to a weekend jumps meeting.

Sprinter Sacre, Bobs Worth and Simonsig have all belied their years and delighted crowds with highly encouraging returns to action in recent weeks. But Cue Card arguably topped the lot of them with a memorably emphatic victory in the Betfair Chase that puts him on course for a possible £1 million payout.

Although he will be ten in five weeks' time, he remains much more Captain Fantastic than Captain Mainwaring on the evidence of his awesome display in the first Grade 1 race of the British jumps season.

Cue Card has long shown himself a horse for the big occasion, whether it be landing the Champion Bumper at Cheltenham in 2010, the Ryanair Chase three years later or this contest two years ago.

There were those who wondered whether his best days might be behind him after a laboured and winless 2014–15 campaign

3.00 Betfair Chase (Registered as The Lancashire Chase) (Grade 1) Class 1 18 fences(3m24y) 3m
[OFF 3.01]
For: 5-y-o and up 1st £112,540 2nd £42,400 3rd £21,220 4th £10,600 5th £5,320

1 **CUE CARD** 9 11-7 t ....(167) **Paddy Brennan**
b g by King's Theatre (IRE)–Wicked Crack (IRE) (King's Ride) (Colin Tizzard) raced with zest mainly in 2nd place, led approaching 3 out, effortlessly went clear before last, easily [bets of £900-£400(x2)] [op 9/4 tchd 13/8] **7/4**

2 7**SILVINIACO CONTI (FR)** 9 11-7 p ......(172) Noel Fehily
ch g by Dom Alco (FR)–Gazelle Lulu (FR) (Altayan) (Paul Nicholls) led, headed approaching 3 out, ridden before 2 out, unable to go with winner before last, no chance after [bets of £800-£500, £1100-£1000, £550-£500, even £3000, even £1500, even £500(px6), £1000-£1100] [op Evens tchd 10/11] **5/4F**

3 t2**DYNASTE (FR)** 9 11-7 tp ....(165) Tom Scudamore
[19] gr g by Martaline–Bellissima de Mai (FR) (Pistolet Bleu (IRE)) (David Pipe) prominent, outpaced when not fluent 3 out, ridden approaching 2 out, lost touch with front two before last [op 8/1] **11/2**

WETHERBY
bet365 Charlie Hall Chase

HAYDOCK
Betfair Chase

2014–15 | 2015–16 | 2016–17 | 2017–18
MAR APR NOV DEC JAN FEB MAR APR NOV DEC JAN FEB MAR APR NOV DEC JAN FEB MAR APR NOV DEC JAN FEB MAR APR

❝

I rode a proper
champion today"

PADDY BRENNAN

but the doubts have been answered by a gutsy chaser who has not put a foot wrong since undergoing an operation to fix a trapped epiglottis.

Although he was receiving weight when starting his campaign with victory in the Charlie Hall Chase at Wetherby, he met dual previous winner Silviniaco Conti at levels yesterday and treated him with disdain.

Paddy Brennan, who landed this race on Imperial Commander in 2010, was happy to track the favourite – albeit an uneasy one, whose price drifted from 10-11 to 5-4 – and moved Cue Card effortlessly into the lead before three out. From there he pulled clear for a seven-length win.

"It's lovely to have him back," said Colin Tizzard, who trains the winner for Jean and Bob Bishop.

"We thought Wetherby was brilliant but we were getting the conditions of the race and today he was taking them all on and he has done it really well.

"The race was set up for him. We wanted to take Silviniaco Conti on before but we used him as a pacemaker, didn't we? We let him do all the work and drag us to the second-last.

"That's class horses for you. They say class is permanent, form is temporary. We've had to deal with his little problems and now he's back to his very best; it's fantastic for us."

Cue Card is now eligible for the £1 million bonus offered for winning this race, the King George and Cheltenham Gold Cup, and Tizzard is committed to having a crack at the jackpot.

"Why would we run away from Kempton?" he said. "There's no reason not to go there. We're the only ones left in the bonus now. If Cue Card's in the form he's in now he'd run in the Gold Cup. That's the ultimate race and he has proved he stays."

Brennan is looking forward to Kempton. "He's the one who is proven," he said. "I knew coming here I wouldn't swap him and I wouldn't swap him for anything in the King George.

"It was some achievement today. We were worried about the ground but it didn't matter what the ground was or the competition, he was unbeatable today. He was unbelievable.

BETFAIR CHASE WINNERS		
Year	Horse	RPR
2015	Cue Card	178
2014	Silviniaco Conti	176
2013	Cue Card	176
2012	Silviniaco Conti	173
2011	Kauto Star	177
2010	Imperial Commander	172
2009	Kauto Star	177
2008	Snoopy Loopy	167
2007	Kauto Star	180
2006	Kauto Star	184

"The great thing about him is that he's learning to settle; that's why he's got a chance of getting the Gold Cup trip. I rode a proper champion today."

Cue Card and Paddy Brennan clear the last fence in the 2015 Betfair Chase at Haydock

RACING POST RATINGS: Cue Card (178+) rolled back the years with a hugely impressive display in yesterday's Betfair Chase and, with his breathing problems seemingly sorted out, he looks sure to be a major player in the King George.

Having failed to fire all last season, Cue Card had looked like he was on the way back when winning on his Wetherby reappearance, but he stepped up significantly on that level of form yesterday and is clearly right back to his best.

HAYDOCK
Betfair Chase

2014–15	2015–16	2016–17	2017–18
MAR APR NOV DEC JAN FEB MAR APR	NOV DEC JAN FEB MAR APR	NOV DEC JAN FEB MAR APR	NOV DEC JAN FEB MAR APR

In his piece from Haydock, Alastair Down highlighted how popular that proper champion had become.

Left: Paddy Brennan punches the air as he returns to the winner's enclosure on Cue Card accompanied by groom Hamir Singh and (above) with Colin Tizzard and their trophies

Certain chasers chisel their way into public affection and, once there, never lose the status of being somehow special.

Tenacity, length of service, heart-on-sleeve effort and sheer talent are all part of their appeal and they become old friends and important members of the jumping family – the sort of horse who, if you're not watching a race through your wallet, you can't help cheering on.

Cue Card is the epitome of the much-loved chaser and he has a proper following. After he had romped to a second Betfair Chase victory at a noisily appreciative Haydock yesterday, that matter-of-fact stockman Colin Tizzard said: "It's lovely to have him back to his very best. It's fantastic for us."

At the risk of picking a fight, Colin, it's fantastic for all of us.

Cue Card was eye-catchingly impressive here under Paddy Brennan, who clearly has an immense amount of time for him. "He was unbelievable," he said, "and it feels like riding a five-year-old – a young one just coming through."

> "He was unbelievable and it feels like riding a five-year-old – a young one just coming through"
>
> **PADDY BRENNAN**

HAYDOCK
Betfair Chase

2014-15						2015-16						2016-17						2017-18					
NOV	DEC	JAN	FEB	MAR	APR	NOV	DEC	JAN	FEB	MAR	APR	NOV	DEC	JAN	FEB	MAR	APR	NOV	DEC	JAN	FEB	MAR	APR

Silviniaco Conti tried to make all but Cue Card headed him three out and sauntered clear. Brennan never had to get so much as half-serious with him and the seven-length margin could have been 17.

Cue Card now joins Sprinter Sacre, Sir Des Champs and Bobs Worth on the growing list of prodigal sons who have returned to illuminate the season.

Last season he had problems with his epiglottis and some other niggles and was beaten in all of his five races. That was not the real Cue Card, who had never before had a longer losing run than three.

For the Tizzards it must have been a massive downer that the apple of their eye was simply not on song. They have such a fierce pride in him and even when you find reasons for a horse being wrong it is never a given that they will come back as good as ever.

Back in June, Cue Card had some pus in a foot and Tizzard used it as an excuse to get him back in as he never does well when the wretched flies are at their worst in July.

In time it became clear the old Cue Card was back and Tizzard said: "Every day all he wants to do is get to the top of that gallop."

It has always struck me that Tizzard has long been itching to run Cue Card in the Gold Cup and it would be mad not to. Time was when Cue Card used to take a fierce tug but he is much more tractable now. Brennan said: "He's learning to settle and that gives him a chance of getting the Gold Cup trip."

Don't forget what a fantastic festival record he has. He won the Champion Bumper, was an excellent fourth to Al Ferof in the Supreme Novices' Hurdle – Sprinter Sacre just ahead in third – second in the Arkle to Sprinter Sacre and bolted up by nine lengths in the Ryanair Chase from one of my heroes, First Lieutenant.

Cheltenham is made for him and he will head that way via the King George at Kempton, where victory would put him in

> "
> Every day all he wants to do is get to the top of that gallop"
>
> **COLIN TIZZARD**

line for the £1 million bonus on the table if he then added the Gold Cup.

Tizzard joked that owner Bob Bishop "has plenty of money already", so maybe the trainer has his eye on a chunk of it. At least that would stop him complaining about the price of milk.

Unsurprisingly in a season with a vintage Gold Cup in prospect, the King George has all the makings of a classic as well with Cue Card appearing from left-field and adding greatly to the mix.

Cue Card has been to three King Georges with little to show for it but in this sort of form he has to be a major player. As Tizzard said: "Why should we run away from Kempton?" Tizzard is not the type of man to run away from anything and his horse of a lifetime is just the same.

It was clear they had their horse back. Joe Tizzard believed he knew why and, speaking to Andrew King two weeks before the King George, observed that Cue Card was simply happier having moved home.

A new stable barn was yesterday revealed as the secret behind the rejuvenation of Cue Card, whose build-up to the King George VI Chase at Kempton on Boxing Day gathered pace when he sparkled in one of his final workouts before an attempt to win the William Hill-backed Grade 1 at the fourth time of asking.

A wind operation has been highlighted as key to his superb wins in the Charlie Hall Chase and Betfair Chase, but Cue Card's plush new accommodation is another huge factor according to the man who knows him best, retired jockey Joe Tizzard – son of trainer Colin – who partnered the nine-year-old 20 times.

Cue Card, along with 51 other horses, is now housed in a brand new stables complex at the yard set high on a hill above the village of Milborne Port.

Tizzard, who assists his father, said of Cue Card: "He seems better than ever and his results this season seem to back that

HAYDOCK
Betfair Chase

2014-15   2015-16   2016-17   2017-18

MAR APR NOV DEC JAN FEB MAR APR NOV DEC JAN FEB MAR APR NOV DEC JAN FEB MAR APR NOV DEC JAN FEB MAR APR

up, as he's always been a bit lazy at home but now he's much more alert, pricking his ears and generally enjoying himself.

"I think the fact the air at the yard is a lot fresher and the whole place is bug-free has been a significant factor in him winning so well at Wetherby and Haydock this season. It's also helped a lot of the others as they are seeing out their races really well – probably better than they were a year ago when they were still stabled down on the farm."

So it was that on Boxing Day he was back at Kempton.

Cue Card had been dazzlingly impressive in the Betfair Chase. That so, it was a mark of the 2015 King George's strength that he was sent off only third best in the betting at 9-2.

Two Irish stars were preferred.

Heading the market at 15-8 was Don Cossack, who had twice thrashed Cue Card in the spring and returned to Britain having won both his new season starts impressively at home.

At 3-1 was the Willie Mullins-trained Vautour, sensational in the JLT Novices' Chase at the Cheltenham Festival and then a smooth winner on his Ascot reappearance.

"It's exciting, nerve-wracking, everything," said Colin Tizzard on the eve of the race.

The same words could have been applied equally to the race itself.

A race with a history full of serial winners fell to one of its multiple losers when the rejuvenated Cue Card fought back ferociously to snatch King George glory at the fourth attempt yesterday, edging out Vautour in a thunderous climax to the Christmas classic.

The race veteran with form figures of 525 in the contest before yesterday finally secured the win he deserved for perseverance alone when rallying under a hard drive from Paddy Brennan, for which he earned an 11-day whip ban and a £4,200 fine, to win a photo-finish verdict by a head.

The result kept alive Cue Card's chances of landing the £1 million Jockey Club Racecourses bonus awarded to con-

3.10   **William Hill King George VI Chase**
[OFF 3.10]   **(Grade 1) Class 1**   18 fences 3m
For: 4-y-o and up 1st £114,436 2nd £43,276 3rd £21,936 4th £11,196 5th £5,896

1   CUE CARD 9 11-10t ....(172) Paddy Brennan
    b g by King's Theatre (IRE)–Wicked Crack (IRE) (King's Ride)
    (Colin Tizzard) tracked leaders, progress 10th, chased leader
    12th, shaken up before 3 out, no impression and just headed for
    2nd when left in it again 2 out, hard ridden and closed last, stayed
    on gamely under pressure to lead post [bets of £2500-£500,
    £4500-£1000, £2250-£500]   [tchd 5/1 in a place] 9/2

2   *hd* VAUTOUR (FR) 6 11-10 ....(171) R Walsh
    b g by Robin Des Champs (FR)–Gazelle de Mai (FR) (Dom
    Pasquini (FR))
    (W P Mullins) tracked leader, led 11th, going best from 4 out, 2
    lengths up 2 out, ridden before last, pressed and driven flat,
    headed post [bet of £2000-£800]
                            [tchd 11/4 and 10/3 in a place] 3/1

3   13 AL FEROF (FR) 10 11-10 ....(165) Harry Skelton
    [13¼] gr g by Dom Alco (FR)–Maralta (FR) (Altayan)
    (Dan Skelton) settled in rear, effort from 12th, took 4th before 3
    out but not on terms with leaders, left 3rd 2 out, no danger
                            [op 20/1] 16/1

nections of a horse who wins the Betfair Chase, William Hill King George VI Chase and Timico Cheltenham Gold Cup.

And the nine-year-old is likely to head straight to the festival without another run, to make his first appearance in the Gold Cup on his fifth run at the fixture.

At the Cheltenham Festival, Cue Card has won the Champion Bumper and Ryanair Chase, but until undergoing surgery on a trapped epiglottis during the summer, he had been repeatedly found wanting in the King George, most frustratingly two years ago when tying up approaching the final fence to be beaten into second by Silviniaco Conti.

When Vautour turned into the straight he looked in complete control.

He was two lengths up at the second-last, when Don Cossack fell, leaving Cue Card the only threat to a sixth King George win for Ruby Walsh. An untidy jump at the last still left Cue Card with ground to make up, but it was the Colin Tizzard stable star who took the spoils.

"Nowadays he's a completely different horse," said Tizzard. "He lobs around in fifth or sixth and looks beaten, and then he has that left for the end. If he'd met the last on a good stride he'd have won by a length and a half.

"He looks like a Gold Cup horse now. At this point I probably think he wouldn't run again because he had a hard race today. He was all out at the line – but it's a very significant fact that now he can finish his races."

He continued: "This win is for the horse. He's been a mainstay of our yard. When he won the Champion Bumper everyone thought I'd trained him too hard as a four-year-old. It just shows they do come back. He was at his brilliant best today. It was a real hot race, and to win it is brilliant.

"Cue Card has been about for a long time and he means everything to me and a lot of other people."

Brennan had a taste of Cheltenham Gold Cup glory on Imperial Commander in 2010, and Cue Card has revived his career.

> **"**
> Cue Card has been about for a long time and he means everything to me and a lot of other people"
> **COLIN TIZZARD**

KEMPTON
William Hill King George VI Chase

2014-15   2015-16   2016-17   2017-18

MAR APR NOV DEC JAN FEB MAR APR NOV DEC JAN FEB MAR APR NOV DEC JAN FEB MAR APR NOV DEC JAN FEB MAR APR

Previous spread: Cue Card (left) at the start before the King George VI Chase at Kempton in December 2015

Above: Cue Card (right) clears the final fence behind Vautour before claiming a famous success in the King George

That's the best feeling of my whole career, the best day of my life"

PADDY BRENNAN

"That's the best feeling of my whole career, the best day of my life," he said. "He's beaten one of the best horses in training; I've beaten one of the best jockeys I've ever ridden against. I'm so proud.

"It was a true race. I'm not going to lie and say there was loads there – I got to the bottom of the tank – but if there's any man that's going to get him back in that kind of form for the Gold Cup it's Colin Tizzard.

"And to the people who say he didn't stay, it's taken him to the line to get there."

Brennan added: "The last time I got in a close finish with Ruby was Imperial Commander against Kauto Star. I thought I'd got there then and I hadn't. Today he said I'd won.

"I'd just like to thank Cue Card, all the staff at Colin Tizzard's, and Bob and Jean Bishop; if it wasn't for them I'd never be in this position."

Although only a narrow winner, Brennan, who took over the ride on Cue Card this season, had been confident of winning beforehand, according to Bob Bishop.

"He rang me yesterday and said, 'I won't sleep a wink tonight because you're going to win tomorrow,'" Bishop revealed.

"When he went to Wetherby, Paddy said the other horses needn't have turned up because we were going to win. Then when we went to the Betfair he said, 'Don't worry about this, go and celebrate because we're going to win it.' The two of them just gel. They are a great partnership.

Paddy Brennan salutes the crowd after Cue Card's thrilling victory in the Boxing Day showpiece

I'd just like to thank Cue Card, all the staff at Colin Tizzard's, and Bob and Jean Bishop; if it wasn't for them I'd never be in this position"

PADDY BRENNAN

KEMPTON
William Hill King George VI Chase

2014–15   2015–16   2016–17   2017–18
MAR | APR | NOV | DEC | JAN | FEB | MAR | APR | NOV | DEC | JAN | FEB | MAR | APR | NOV | DEC | JAN | FEB | MAR | APR | NOV | DEC | JAN | FEB | MAR | APR

"Winning the Betfair Chase was great, but today must be the best moment. It's the tops."

RACING POST RATINGS: Cue Card (180) posted a career-best performance to land a thrilling William Hill King George VI Chase, in the process recording the best winning RPR since Kauto Star registered the last of his five wins in 2011.

He had looked certain to collect jumping the second-last fence in this race two years ago, while this time around he looked third best approaching the same fence.

Bob and Jean Bishop with Paddy Brennan and Colin Tizzard with the King George VI Chase trophy

Alastair Down was every bit as enthused.

Rightly popular, plucky to his very marrow and a paragon among chasers, Cue Card gave his all to win a pulsating King George under a ride of uncompromising severity from Paddy Brennan.

Cue Card and Vautour passed the post almost as one, but the judge speedily announced that Colin Tizzard's wonderful stalwart had won the King George at the fourth time of asking and the news was greeted with a vast blast of acclaim from the Kempton crowd.

Ruby Walsh led at the 11th with a mile to run and was still two lengths to the good when the complexion of the race changed at the second-last.

Favourite Don Cossack, the gamble of the race, had ground himself back into contention and was lying second and sticking on grimly when falling at that penultimate obstacle.

In all frankness he was not travelling with any ease or fluency on the second circuit and did well to get back into the fight. His departure left Cue Card in second and you could almost see Brennan sensing all was not lost and the tiger beneath him was still in with a shout.

And there was nothing Brennan did not ask from Cue Card. On the run to the final fence his whip fell five times on his mount and, while Cue Card responded to his core they were still a good length down at the last, where both principals made a mistake.

Walsh wasn't playing pat-a-cake on Vautour but, suddenly, with Brennan in full cry, Cue Card was hauling him back in and stuck his head in front on the line.

Cue Card is something of a legend. There are strong rumours in the racing village that one of Tizzard's rival training establishments recently approached owners Bob and Jean Bishop with an offer to train that legend on what might politely be called advantageous terms.

Trying to get Cue Card off Tizzard is without any doubt flirting with a near-death experience. No, make that certain

KING GEORGE WINNERS BY RPR		
Year	Winner	RPR
2015	Cue Card	180
2014	Silviniaco Conti	175
2013	Silviniaco Conti	177
2012	Long Run	174
2011	Kauto Star	182
2010	Long Run	181
2009	Kauto Star	191
2008	Kauto Star	181
2007	Kauto Star	184
2006	Kauto Star	180

KEMPTON
William Hill King George VI Chase

death. Colin would rather get rid of his wife and children than be parted from Cue Card.

Stockmen such as Tizzard are not given to sentiment when it comes to animals, but there is no doubt Cue Card has got past Colin's defences as he simply loves this horse. And he is not alone.

Cue Card has had some benchmark days – not least two Betfair Chases – but this was the zenith as Boxing Day has not been festive for him in years past and there will have been some glum drives home to the Dorset/Somerset border.

But this afternoon paid for all, and Tizzard said: "We're being a bit more careful with the good horses now. We used to try to get them super, super-fit but the new way of doing things seems to suit them. Dreams are made of days like this.

"He's had a hard race today and was all out at the line," and that entirely accurate assessment was backed up by Brennan, who said: "Ruby wasn't stopping, I can tell you, and we needed every yard out there."

On the night of the King George, Bob and Jean Bishop returned home to Bexhill and celebrated. Cue Card had given them so many unforgettable days, but none, according to Bob, had been better than this one.

"We've had some really good times, but that was the best," he said, following what he admitted had been "a rather late" night.

"We knew he had tremendous ability, but he wasn't finishing the races and didn't at times look very happy. Two years ago in the King George it looked from two out he'd the race won, but then he started to choke. We've had the epiglottis operation, which seems to have worked wonders.

"The plan is to go to Cheltenham, but there are some good horses. I'm sure everyone who owns a National Hunt horse wants to win the Gold Cup – and we're certainly no different."

Praising Cue Card's rider, Bishop added: "Paddy rode for us and won for us in the past. We've always had a great admiration for him as a jockey. When Joe packed up I rang Paddy to see how he was

"

Dreams are made of days like this"

COLIN TIZZARD

Cue Card and Hamir Singh at
Colin Tizzard's Venn Farm stables
in February 2016

fixed for the following season, but he was well ensconced with Tom George so Daryl Jacob rode Cue Card.

"I'm feeling sorry for Daryl because Cue Card wasn't at his best last year because of the wind problem. When it looked like Daryl wasn't available this season I got a call from Paddy and he asked if the offer was still open. I said it was and we talked to Colin, and the horse and Paddy are completely one – they gel."

KEMPTON
William Hill King George VI Chase

2014-15   2015-16   2016-17   2017-18

MAR | APR | NOV | DEC | JAN | FEB | MAR | APR | NOV | DEC | JAN | FEB | MAR | APR | NOV | DEC | JAN | FEB | MAR | APR | NOV | DEC | JAN | FEB | MAR | APR

Colin Tizzard with his stable stars
Cue Card (left) and Thistlecrack. There
was a friendly rivalry between the two
sets of owners

On the possibility of scooping the owner's £650,000 chunk of the £1m Jockey Club bonus, he said: "You might not believe me, but it's never mentioned. It's a big ask and the horse doesn't owe us one penny."

The next time Bob Bishop's name appeared in the Racing Post was to report his death. He passed away on Wednesday, December 30.

Bob Bishop, joint-owner of the hugely popular King George VI Chase hero Cue Card, died aged 83 on Wednesday night, just four days after the superstar jumper gave him the highlight of his racing life.

Bishop raced Cue Card in the colours of wife Jean, who lost her husband of 62 years on her own birthday and who yesterday described their association with the dual Cheltenham Festival winner as "perfect".

The leading Gold Cup fancy's trainer Colin Tizzard remembered Bishop, also survived by daughters Janice and Lesley, as the "straightest, fairest man" he had ever met.

"We're all speechless because it happened so suddenly," said Jean Bishop.

"He was taken to hospital at 8.30am on Wednesday. During the afternoon he had difficulty breathing and we were later told he was very ill with kidney failure. A chaplain said a few prayers and we were all with him until he passed away."

She added: "We have been in racing a long time and the last six years have been perfect for us. Cue Card has given us so much pleasure and we were both so lucky to have him. When things go right in racing there is nothing like it.

"All our wins have been special but the King George was extra special. We felt privileged just to have a horse good enough to run in the race. We didn't even think we had won it. Another of Colin's owners came over to us straight after the race and said, 'Well done.' Bob thanked him and said it was good the horse had finished second, only to be told Cue Card hadn't come second but had won. We now have lovely memories of that day."

The Bishops had horses together for 30 years, initially with Fulke Walwyn, and for the last six years have enjoyed great success with Tizzard and his son Joe, their former regular rider.

Colin Tizzard said: "King George day was one of the most exciting, exhilarating days any of us associated with Cue Card have ever had. Bob was in good form at Kempton and we had spoken every day since, so his death has come as a great shock.

"Bob was the straightest, fairest man I've ever met. He had an amazing life as well. He was once a professional footballer, he worked for the police and he was an investigator of major insurance claims and he even negotiated with kidnappers. He loved to tell me about his travels around the world and the characters he met."

Paddy Brennan, in the saddle this season for Cue Card's King George triumph, his second success in the Betfair Chase and prior to that his win in the Charlie Hall Chase, said: "Bob Bishop was an absolute gentleman. I told him I would win him the King George and I'm now even prouder I did. He was so easy to speak to and so genuine. We'll all miss him."

> We have been in racing a long time and the last six years have been perfect for us"
>
> **JEAN BISHOP**

Bob and Jean Bishop on Boxing Day night 2015 with their great-grandchildren Daisy, Molly, Sophie and Stanley sitting in the King George VI trophy

Brennan now had an extra reason for wanting to win the Gold Cup. A driven character, he had forged a tremendous partnership with Cue Card. He longed to give Jean Bishop reason to smile at Cheltenham.

"I'll be doing it for Bob, he'll be behind me," said Brennan in mid-February, while also admitting the extra £100,000 that would come to him as the jockey's slice of the Jockey Club loot was not to be sniffed at.

"Of course the bonus is in my thoughts," he said. "Every race you ride in there is pressure and you have to get it right. The first and foremost thing on my mind will be going out there to keep it as simple as possible, not to panic. If it does come off it will be unbelievable."

It did not come off. It failed to come off in the most spectacularly dramatic fashion.

In the betting, Don Cossack and Cue Card had been practically inseparable, the former setting off as 9-4 favourite with Cue Card at 5-2. Running down the Cheltenham hill towards the third-last fence they were similarly inseparable.

Cue Card was cruising when it happened. Brennan had moved him forward, in between the rail-running Djakadam and Don Cossack. Britain's big hope took off fractionally in front but he failed to take off enough. It was a horrendous mistake, one from which he stood no chance of recovering. The main blessing was he was quickly back on his feet as his stunned rider sank to his knees, head in his hands and suffered.

Don Cossack went on to win the Gold Cup – the Gold Cup so many thought Cue Card could, should and would have won but for falling. He had never once fallen before.

On Gold Cup Friday, Brennan felt unable to talk about how he felt. One day later the words came pouring out of him.

Cue Card's costly tumble in the Timico Cheltenham Gold Cup is something Paddy Brennan will likely never get over, the rider said yesterday when he opened his heart about the disappointment of the ten-year-old's fall.

Opposite: Paddy Brennan works Cue Card at Kempton Park in February 2016 in preparation for a first tilt at the Cheltenham Gold Cup

2009-10   2010-11   2011-12   2012-13   2013-14

JAN | FEB | MAR | APR | NOV | DEC | JAN | FEB | MAR | APR | NOV | DEC | JAN | FEB | MAR | APR | NOV | DEC | JAN | FEB | MAR | APR | NOV | DEC | JAN | FEB

CHELTENHAM
Timico Cheltenham
Gold Cup Chase

2014–15   2015–16   2016–17   2017–18

MAR | APR | NOV | DEC | JAN | FEB | MAR | APR | NOV | DEC | JAN | FEB | MAR | APR | NOV | DEC | JAN | FEB | MAR | APR | NOV | DEC | JAN | FEB | MAR | APR

"

Who knows if he would
have won – but what
I do know is when I
jumped into that gap
I felt like I was on a
very fresh horse"

PADDY BRENNAN

Trained by Colin Tizzard for Jean Bishop, the popular Cue Card – who won the Champion Bumper in 2010 and Ryanair Chase in 2013 – was in line to land a £1 million bonus on Friday if he added the Gold Cup to his Betfair Chase and King George triumphs, but he fell when challenging winner Don Cossack and runner-up Djakadam three from home.

Tizzard, who reported the son of King's Theatre to be 100 per cent fine yesterday morning, was not fussed about missing out on the money, and neither was Brennan, who was left to ponder what might have been.

The jockey, who offered his congratulations to Don Cossack's connections, said: "I jumped the one at the top of the hill and, as Noel Fehily was dropping back on O'Faolains Boy and I was just starting to niggle Cue Card, I dared him into a gap between Djakadam and Don Cossack to see how he'd react.

"I promise you he started running away with me. He came alive."

Brennan went on: "We met that fence on no stride. It's very hard to explain. His jumping has always been A1, but the fact he got in among them and latched on to the bridle I think took me by surprise, maybe him by surprise.

"In hindsight, you might have done something different. You might not have put him into the gap, but I did because I wasn't sure how he was going and once I did he started running away with me. He was only getting going and I was confident he'd get the trip. I felt if I had got over that fence I'd have been able to sit and wait around the bend and gone on to win.

"Who knows if he would have won – it was three out – but what I do know is when I jumped into that gap I felt I was on a very fresh horse."

Brennan added: "It's the hardest thing I've had to put myself through for sure. I'm probably more disappointed for Colin and Jean and her late husband Bob than I am for myself. Everything was going to plan and we ended up on the ground. It's probably something I'll never get over, but I'm a firm believer you've got to move forward.

"I'll never forget the days he won at Haydock and Kempton, but I'll certainly never forget yesterday. We got so close, yet were so far away."

Tizzard said: "We trotted him out this morning and he went for a bite of grass and was 100 per cent fine.

"He was bright and happy and you can see he didn't have a hard race because it ended so abruptly. I couldn't be happier with him. There's not a scratch on him.

"He runs differently to what he used to and travels just behind the bridle nowadays. He made that move and was just in front at the time, hard on the steel. It was lovely and then two seconds later he was gone. We'll never know, but he was running a big race and I'm sure he would've been heavily involved.

"I can't say I'm disappointed for me; I'm disappointed for the horse because he's been brilliant for us for a long time and it would've been great for him to prove he was capable of winning a Gold Cup. It would've been great, but at least everything is fine and we can have another day."

That day would be at Aintree on the opening afternoon of the Grand National festival.

Prior to the Merseyside trip, Paddy Brennan had visited the Tizzards and schooled Cue Card.

"He jumped immaculately, brilliant," said Colin Tizzard. "He was up a bit higher, like he remembered the fall. He wasn't guessy or anything, he was just making sure."

The fences on Aintree's Mildmay course take a lot of jumping. Cue Card jumped them beautifully, hitting one fence but neither then nor at any point in the race looking vulnerable. He was sent off 6-5 favourite for the Betfred Bowl but won it like a long odds-on shot. Gold Cup second Djakadam, beaten four and a half lengths by Don Cossack at Cheltenham, was this time 17 lengths inferior to Cue Card.

If ever there was a horse guaranteed to put a smile on your face it is Cue Card – no wonder they were cheering as he returned to the winner's enclosure.

CHELTENHAM
Timico Cheltenham Gold
Cup Chase

AINTREE
Betfred Bowl Chase

| | 2014-15 | | | | | | | 2015-16 | | | | | 2016-17 | | | | | | 2017-18 | | | | |
| MAR | APR | NOV | DEC | JAN | FEB | MAR | APR | NOV | DEC | JAN | FEB | MAR | APR | NOV | DEC | JAN | FEB | MAR | APR | NOV | DEC | JAN | FEB | MAR | APR |

> Cue Card proved how special he is and how special his connections are. They never doubted me"

PADDY BRENNAN

And no one can blame Paddy Brennan for punching the air in delight after a redemptive victory that was as much a relief as a triumph.

Cue Card has been a source of delight since he ended Irish domination of the Cheltenham Bumper with a 40-1 triumph six years ago, racing with boundless enthusiasm that is positively infectious.

There have been numerous highs since, in a career that has taken in victories in two Betfair Chases, a Ryanair and a King George.

There have also been lows, none more galling than at Cheltenham last month when he fell at the third-last fence in the Gold Cup just as he was poised to deliver a challenge that might have earned his connections a £1 million bonus.

Nobody felt the disappointment more than Brennan, who has formed such a formidable partnership with the rejuvenated ten-year-old this season.

"If a horse falls, nine times out of ten a jockey is going to blame himself," said the rider, who admitted it had not been easy to live with the thought of what might have been.

"You wake up at three in the morning and it's not a nice feeling. I wouldn't wish it on anybody."

But Cue Card has made a career of bouncing back from adversity – his memorable campaign has come on the back of a disappointing 2014–15 when he failed to win a race.

And he showed no trace of his jolting Cheltenham experience as he lifted the Betfred Bowl with a peerless display to delight Brennan, trainer Colin Tizzard and owner Jean Bishop, enjoying the chaser's first success since her husband Bob died a few days after the King George.

He moved smoothly into the lead after the third-last to score by nine lengths from the Gold Cup third Don Poli, with Cheltenham runner-up Djakadam another eight lengths further back.

"There's a lot of relief," Brennan admitted. "Everyone will have their opinion about Cheltenham, but that's the game.

Paddy Brennan gives Cue Card a well-deserved pat as they stroll home in front of Don Poli and Djakadam (left) to win the Betfred Bowl at Aintree in April 2016

"There's been criticism but the support has been unbelievable. And in racing you walk out of the Gold Cup and start again the next day, you move on."

Brennan, who had taken this race on Nacarat for Tom George in 2011, was quick to pay tribute to the faith Cue Card's connections had shown in him.

"Cue Card proved how special he is and how special his connections are," he said. "They never doubted me. The Tizzards and Bishops have been fully behind me and I didn't feel

AINTREE
Betfred Bowl Chase

> I think we might have won the Gold Cup, but you've got to jump the fences and he didn't at Cheltenham"

COLIN TIZZARD

any pressure today because I knew he was fresh and I knew he would love the track. The only thing it leaves me thinking is that I probably would have won at Cheltenham. But we'll enjoy today and hopefully he can win the Gold Cup next year."

But before then there could be a trip to Ireland.

The trainer said: "He's in the form of his life and we're not stopping yet, we're going to Punchestown. There are lots of times in a horse's life when you can't run them because they're not right, but he's right at the top of his game."

Tizzard was delighted to see Cue Card set the record straight with the seventh Grade 1 success of his career.

"This was fantastic. It was so disappointing at Cheltenham and I'm just proud of the horse. It's a brilliant day. The real pleasure of it all is he's ten now and better than he's ever been. It was a brilliant performance today. I think we might have won the Gold Cup but you've got to jump the fences and he didn't at Cheltenham." (David Carr)

RACING POST RATINGS: From a ratings perspective, day one of Aintree more than lived up to expectations with Cue Card (RPR 180+) topping the bill with a performance out of the top drawer.

Rated 180 when getting up to deny Vautour in the King George, Cue Card found things easier yesterday and, with Gold Cup runner-up Djakadam (164) running below form in third, he proved far too classy for Don Poli (168) who looks to have at least reproduced his festival mark.

It was too far out to say if Cue Card would have beaten Don Cossack (182) when falling at the third-last in the Gold Cup, but yesterday's performance did nothing to dispel the notion it would have been a good finish.

Also at Aintree to see the Cue Card stroll was Alastair Down.

To a degree, all those close to Cue Card will ever be haunted by the third-last at Cheltenham, but the old warrior was at his born-again brilliant best in the Betfred Bowl.

The Gold Cup ghost was not laid to rest here, but it was exorcised for a while by a result greeted with widespread delight and the feeling that a degree of justice had been done.

Having led three out, Cue Card travelled in the first-class seats here with the others scrubbing away in steerage. He simply danced home and was eased heavily in the final 100 yards to knock Don Poli and Djakadam cold by nine lengths and eight.

All season Colin Tizzard has been insisting Cue Card has been in the form of his life and he has been right all along, because the ten-year-old, with a genuinely glittering back catalogue of achievement, has raised himself to another level.

Doubtless in the privacy of his own home, Tizzard has kicked the odd door and railed at the fates. But his public handling of what must have been an agonising reverse has been exemplary. Nothing gnaws away at you quite like a might-have-been and that sort of chance rarely, if ever, knocks twice.

Paddy Brennan is unable to contain his delight after winning the 2016 Betfred Bowl on Cue Card

AINTREE
Betfred Bowl Chase

But farmers have to be phlegmatic and tough by necessity. They deal with animals, and as Dick Hern once said: "If you have livestock you have dead stock."

Tizzard knows Cheltenham could have been even more dire, and said: "It was the one that got away. Thank God he got up – because they don't all get up, do they?

"I never thought he'd fall and he'd never been on the ground before. It probably wasn't wasted on him."

And if you want a measure of the man it came from Paddy Brennan, who said: "At Kempton, the day after the Gold Cup, he came up, gave me a pat on the back and said, 'The horse is fine – we're going to Aintree.'"

No tortuous post mortems or dramas, just a simple confidence-boosting sentence that equally meant, "You're going to Aintree."

Brennan is a complex character, perhaps too savage on himself when running events through the card index of memory. He will have been through plenty of dark nights of the soul since the festival and this has to have been a restorative afternoon.

Asked what Cue Card meant to him he simply answered, "everything", and made it clear that in terms of "pressure and self-esteem", this victory was as important and rewarding as any in his career.

It is understandable Cue Card means everything to Brennan, but he also means a hell of a lot to the jumps public and his welcome back to the winner's enclosure was warm, sustained and heartfelt.

He returned with a nasty-looking lump low on his near fore, but at present the plan is onwards and upwards to the end-of-term party at Punchestown.

For the Cue Card camp that proved to be a pretty tame party.

"We pretend we know everything, but at this time of year you never quite know how a horse will run," said Colin Tizzard prior to the Punchestown Gold Cup. He had been right to be cautious. For although the British raider was much the best horse in the race on figures, he underperformed in fourth, the season's exertions finally taking their toll.

Yet what a season it had been, one full of ups and one notable down. Cue Card had resurrected his career and dug ever deeper into the hearts of racing fans.

AINTREE
Betfred Bowl Chase

PUNCHESTOWN
Bibby Financial Services Ireland
Punchestown Gold Cup

2014-15 | 2015-16 | 2016-17 | 2017-18

MAR | APR | NOV | DEC | JAN | FEB | MAR | APR | NOV | DEC | JAN | FEB | MAR | APR | NOV | DEC | JAN | FEB | MAR | APR | NOV | DEC | JAN | FEB | MAR | APR

5
FINAL FLOURISH

Previous spread: Paddy Brennan and Cue Card
clear the final fence in the 2017 Ascot Chase

ALL THOSE associated with Cue Card went into the new season feeling hopeful. The Tizzards had twice as many reasons to feel that way.

For although the 2016 Cheltenham Festival had been cruel to all those connected with Cue Card, the now veteran's trainer had enjoyed one of the biggest successes of his career one day earlier when Thistlecrack destroyed the opposition in what is now the Stayers' Hurdle.

It seemed highly likely the paths of the stablemates would soon cross. Despite never having jumped a fence in public, Thistlecrack was 7-1 favourite for the Gold Cup after connections made clear that, should all go well, he would be aimed at jumping's most prestigious prize, as opposed to the novices' version, the RSA Chase.

For Cue Card, a second assault on the Gold Cup was also the prime objective – and having narrowly missed out on a £1 million windfall, the bonus was again on their minds.

"You're always hoping, always dreaming in this sport, and although I'm not saying he's going to be a better horse, there's nothing to say he won't be every bit as good," said Paddy Brennan shortly before Cue Card's seasonal reappearance.

"The really good thing about the bonus," he added, "is it attracted the attention of people who don't usually take an interest in racing. They started asking questions about the bonus and it helped Cue Card become the people's horse."

The first question asked of the people's horse was on the familiar turf of Wetherby, where his 2015–16 campaign had started so well with a win. The campaign started well again, this time not with a win but an encouragingly solid run, as I witnessed on a trip to Yorkshire.

Defeated but not deflated. That was the reaction of trainer Colin Tizzard to the reappearance effort of Cue Card, who finished an honourable third in his bid to complete back-to-back victories in the bet365 Charlie Hall Chase.

Twelve months ago, Wetherby's showpiece prize was the launch pad to a sensational season for Cue Card, who went on to win the Betfair Chase, King George VI Chase and Betfred

Bowl, but fell three out in the Timico Cheltenham Gold Cup when still cruising alongside eventual winner Don Cossack.

Connections were planning a similar route for the ten-year-old before the Charlie Hall and they still are, with Jean Bishop's star now bound for Haydock's Grade 1 feature, for which the sponsor has him as favourite at 2-1, having pushed him out from 6-4.

"I thought he ran a fantastic race – it was a horse race and we're not going to win them all," said Tizzard, although for much of the Charlie Hall, Cue Card did seem set to win. However, after racing prominently throughout, he got weary in the closing stages and took third behind Irish Cavalier and Menorah.

"I thought he was going to win but he just got tired in the end," said Tizzard.

"You never quite know first time out. We did give him the racecourse gallop as I didn't want to come here and wish I'd done it, but he has had a good blow.

"The winner had a race three weeks ago and they wouldn't have left anything in Menorah's locker as he doesn't handle heavy ground. I would sooner he'd won but I'm still absolutely delighted with him."

He was indeed delighted, but the more Colin Tizzard thought about the Charlie Hall, the more he thought the tactics used on Cue Card had been wrong. He was quick to admit they had been the tactics he had told Brennan to deploy.

On reflection, he believed the horse had been ridden too aggressively, in effect setting sail for home sooner than might have been desirable. Tizzard therefore publicly stated that when Cue Card made his latest foray to Haydock he would be ridden with more restraint. Given the Betfair Chase field was set to include habitual front-runner and former Cheltenham Gold Cup hero Coneygree, that looked like being perfectly possible.

Cue Card and Coneygree made it to the Haydock starting tape, Cue Card beginning the race as 15-8 favourite, a smidgeon ahead

> **"**
> I would sooner he'd won but I'm still absolutely delighted with him"
>
> **COLIN TIZZARD**

WETHERBY
bet365 Charlie Hall Chase

		2014-15						2015-16						2016-17						2017-18				
MAR	APR	NOV	DEC	JAN	FEB	MAR	APR	NOV	DEC	JAN	FEB	MAR	APR	NOV	DEC	JAN	FEB	MAR	APR	NOV	DEC	JAN	FEB	MAR	APR

3.00   **Betfair Chase (Grade 1)**
[OFF 3.01]   **(Registered As The Lancashire**
Chase) Class 1   18 fences(3m24y) 3m
For: 5-y-o and up 1st £119,689.08 2nd £46,392.77 3rd £24,259.67 4th £13,161.77

1   **CUE CARD** 10 11-7 † ....(176) **Paddy Brennan**
b g by King's Theatre (IRE)–Wicked Crack (IRE) (King's Ride
(IRE))
(Colin Tizzard) held up, handy 4th, went 2nd 11th, big jump 12th,
led approaching 4 out, soon in command, drew clear from 2 out,
driven out and stayed on well [bets of £8000-£4000,
£4000-£2000, £1000-£500, £3750-£2000, £1500-£800,
£750-£400, £750-£400]   [tchd 2/1] **15/8F**

2   15 **CONEYGREE** 9 11-7 ....(170) Richard Johnson
b g by Karinga Bay–Plaid Maid (IRE) (Executive Perk)
(Mark Bradstock) led, headed approaching 4 out, ridden before 3
out, one pace before 2 out, unable to go with winner after [bet of
£1063-£500]   [op 9/4 tchd 5/2] **2/1**

3   13 **VEZELAY** (FR) 7 11-7 † ¹ ....Felix de Giles
[28] b g by Dom Alco (FR)–Outre Mer (FR) (Sleeping Car (FR))
(Emmanuel Clayeux) held up, headway to chase leaders
approaching 10th, went 3rd before 4 out, no impression on front
two   **50/1**

of 2-1 shot Coneygree. With fellow Betfair Chase regular Silviniaco Conti also fancied to run well, this was another rock-solid Grade 1 prize.

It was won with ease. Cue Card's love affair with Haydock was about to be strengthened. Earlier in the week, Paddy Brennan had ridden his 1,000th career winner. I was able to write for the Racing Post that his week got even better.

Cold winter days at Haydock have regularly served up fare to send racegoers home toasty warm and a track synonymous with great staying chasers did so yet again as Cue Card, surely the most popular horse in training, produced a magnificent performance to win a magnificent race.

Public affection for Cue Card and Coneygree is huge, and rightly so, but the durability, consistency and talent of the Colin Tizzard-trained veteran has taken him to the very heart of racing fans.

At the age of ten, rising 11, he showed exactly why when bouncing back from a Wetherby defeat to secure his third Betfair Chase success in a gripping contest that left the winner and runner-up covered in glory and the connections of both horses justifiably delighted.

On ground turned heavy by persistent rain and sleet, this eagerly awaited encounter was never going to be pretty. It nonetheless conjured up a beautiful sight as the evergreen Cue Card and 2015 Gold Cup hero Coneygree fought out a stirring battle up Haydock's home straight.

With the Bradstocks' brittle but brilliant warrior not surprisingly tested for fitness in the closing stages having attempted to make all, it was Cue Card and Paddy Brennan who powered to a 15-length victory after taking the lead at the top of the home straight.

Jubilant trainer Colin Tizzard had been stuck in a traffic jam on the way to the track but he was thrilled to witness one-way traffic in the closing stages of a prize his champion had previously won in 2013 and 2015.

Cue Card is out on his own when winning the 2016 Betfair Chase from Coneygree (centre) at Haydock

"He absolutely sluiced up today," said Tizzard. "He's every bit as good as he ever has been. He didn't have a hard race at all, did he?" Cue Card will have a chance to prove his trainer right about that when charged with following up his 2015 triumph in the 32Red King George VI Chase, for which the sponsors make him 7-4 favourite, one place in front of 4-1 shot Coneygree.

From Kempton it will be on to the home of jumping where, but for an agonising fall at the third-last fence, Cue Card might well in March have claimed the Timico Cheltenham Gold Cup and Jockey Club Racecourses' £1 million Chase Triple Crown bonus.

Standing in his way at the festival could well be stablemate and 4-1 Gold Cup favourite Thistlecrack. While he has run only twice over fences, Cue Card was yesterday doing so for the 26th time, and this was his 15th strike in a career in which he first achieved fame by winning the Weatherbys Champion Bumper seven seasons ago.

One of the races he did not win was last month's Charlie Hall Chase, but that had not knocked Tizzard's confidence.

"He blew for 45 minutes afterwards," he said, recalling the Wetherby run. "He likes this ground. Three years ago we'd have been worried about it but the few times we have run him on it he has floated on top.

"He's got the best place in the stable. He can look out and see everybody. He deserves that. He's a star."

> **"**
> He's got the best place in the stable. He can look out and see everybody. He deserves that. He's a star"
>
> **COLIN TIZZARD**

HAYDOCK
Betfair Chase

Paddy Brennan punches the air when crossing the line in the Betfair Chase

"

I've never been associated with a horse who is so attached to the people and the crowd. I can't wait to ride him again"

PADDY BRENNAN

Owner Jean Bishop would certainly agree. "I suppose it gets more special each time," she said, while Brennan, who entered the Cue Card story at the start of last season, was equally overjoyed.

"He's magnificent," he said. "The way he jumped and travelled was exceptional.

"The ground was way too quick for him at Wetherby but I knew I was on the best horse today and he pretty much annihilated them.

"I've never been associated with a horse who is so attached to the people and the crowd. I can't wait to ride him again."

And the people can't wait to see him.

Six days after the retirement of Sprinter Sacre on what became a desperately difficult afternoon, the sport was in need of a boost. A wonderful old horse delivered it. Right on cue.

2009-10   2010-11   2011-12   2012-13   2013-14

JAN | FEB | MAR | APR | NOV | DEC | JAN | FEB | MAR | APR | NOV | DEC | JAN | FEB | MAR | APR | NOV | DEC | JAN | FEB | MAR | APR | NOV | DEC | JAN | FEB

Right on cue with some wonderful words was Alastair Down, who revealed he also had a role in Cue Card's third Betfair Chase triumph – not as big a role as Brennan or Tizzard, but a role nonetheless.

Brian Hughes (left) on Seeyouatmidnight and Jonathan Moore on Irish Cavalier congratulate Paddy Brennan after Cue Card's Betfair Chase success

Long a living National Hunt treasure, Cue Card continues to delight and astound in equal measure and his third Betfair Chase win in front of a hugely happy Haydock crowd ensures that there is a corner of Lancashire that will forever be part of Dorset.

But there was more to this Betfair than Cue Card further cementing his already close relationship with the public because although Coneygree was beaten 15 lengths into second, you could not have asked much more from a comeback run.

The 2015 Gold Cup winner – and never forget how he ripped that field apart – is back in business and the Bradstocks, fuelled by a bullish Dickie Johnson, were delighted.

HAYDOCK
Betfair Chase

2014-15   2015-16   2016-17   2017-18

MAR | APR | NOV | DEC | JAN | FEB | MAR | APR | NOV | DEC | JAN | FEB | MAR | APR | NOV | DEC | JAN | FEB | MAR | APR | NOV | DEC | JAN | FEB | MAR | APR

"

That was his best ever and he keeps surprising me. With some give underfoot it is dangerous what he can do"

PADDY BRENNAN

But this was Cue Card's day – as it has been on seemingly countless occasions since he trounced his festival bumper rivals by eight lengths as a four-year-old, which feels so long ago it must have been shown in black and white.

Age has never wearied him nor the passage of years tarnished either his allure or sheer ability. As Colin Tizzard, having a cloud nine season, said: "He is every bit as good as he has ever been and time is not catching up with him."

Some will tell you that a three-mile grind through the Haydock heavy is not a thing of beauty but, of course, they are completely wrong because the sight of Coneygree trying to draw the sting from Cue Card was compelling.

This was steeplechasing in the raw with Coneygree making the running as expected and throwing in some mighty leaps with plenty of air to spare. He would have jumped the fearsome Haydock fences of old just as contemptuously.

Last year's Gold Cup winner, who is all potency and threat, stuck to his task in front but Paddy Brennan must have swallowed an extra handful of chill pills and was never in the slightest hurry, sticking to the old inside-hare route and biding his time as he knew he was sitting on oceans of reserve.

He took closer order on Cue Card just under a mile out and you knew that although Coneygree wasn't struggling, his measure was about to be taken.

Cue Card led going to the fourth-last and from then on it was all about standing up and taking the happy acclaim from the stands. This crowd admires Coneygree and wanted him back, but they love Cue Card as one of their own.

In command up the straight he came home alone and adored.

Brennan punched the air passing the post and then fell affectionately on the horse's neck. He was unstinting in his praise and said: "That was his best ever and he keeps surprising me. With some give underfoot it is dangerous what he can do."

Part of his delight on Saturday was that Cue Card was throwing wide open an all-important window of opportunity.

I am a Brennan fan but nobody would pretend that he is not a complex fellow and you know that the third-last in the Gold Cup must occasionally play the monkey and leap on his back.

Tell him 1,000 times it was not his fault and it will matter not a jot. Cue Card, rampant on Saturday, tells Paddy that the fire still burns hot as ever and that means there is a chance of righting a wrong.

The Americans have a saying 'and justice for all' and a Gold Cup would be just that – for Cue Card, Tizzard, Brennan and everyone in the islands for whom the great chasers give life extra meaning and depth.

Truth be told, there would have been no Betfair Chase triumph for Brennan but for your correspondent's heroic rescue act at Keele services or some such horrendous motorway stopover.

Having paused on the trek north for a double espresso, I was getting into the car when Paddy suddenly appeared in the car park and said: "Alastair, I need a lift. There are two of us."

I was tempted to say, 'Why do you need a lift? Got a decent ride somewhere?' But thought better of it.

So Messrs Brennan and Jamie Bargary were loaded into the car as they had managed, with the help of Alain Cawley, to do something not very bright with Paddy's shiny Merc in the car park, involving a wheel and a raised kerb. The score was Kerb 1 – Merc 0. It is fine licensing jockeys to ride horses but the truth is that they should not be allowed to drive cars.

So I was the AA yesterday – that's Automobile Association rather than the other AA, with whose work I am also familiar – and duly delivered two jockeys to Haydock where both rode winners.

If Brennan had not got there who knows whether Cue Card would have won with some strange rider on his back? I would never want anything so vulgar as money – perish the thought – but should Cue Card win the £1 million bonus, a small consideration around the ten per cent mark would be appreciated. No, make that grabbed.

HAYDOCK
Betfair Chase

2014–15   2015–16   2016–17   2017–18
MAR   APR   NOV   DEC   JAN   FEB   MAR   APR   NOV   DEC   JAN   FEB   MAR   APR   NOV   DEC   JAN   FEB   MAR   APR   NOV   DEC   JAN   FEB   MAR   APR

David Carr was also part of the Racing Post's Haydock team and spoke to the winning rider, a man plainly besotted with Cue Card.

Perhaps now the man himself will start to believe what we've all thought for quite a while – he really is some jockey.

When Paddy Brennan rode the 1,000th winner of his career at Warwick this week, the most striking thing was his humility at joining the pantheon of jump racing greats alongside Tony McCoy, Richard Dunwoody and other distinguished riders.

He stressed that he "never thought I was blessed with that much talent" and reckoned himself "an example to young jockeys that anything is achievable as long as you work hard".

But Brennan's effort on Cue Card proved once again, not that any more proof was needed, that this is a rider who can get the job done on the biggest occasions.

He showed that all those years ago on Inglis Drever in his days with Howard Johnson, confirmed it on Nigel Twiston-Davies' Imperial Commander in the Cheltenham Gold Cup and has scarcely put a foot wrong on the Grade 1 stage since teaming up with Cue Card just over a year ago.

Typically, he might beg to differ, pointing to the fall three out that robbed the burgeoning partnership of Gold Cup glory in March.

And equally typically he directed the cheers to his victorious mount as the crowd stood and roared on his return to the winner's enclosure after they repeated last year's Betfair Chase success.

But you don't ride 1,000 winners on hard work alone and Brennan deserved the plaudits after he judged things perfectly, taking the canniest route on the inside rail, never allowing Coneygree too much rope, heading him four out and scoring with authority.

Yet the rider was quick to pay tribute to the way Cue Card's trainer had coaxed so much improvement out of the ten-year-old since his third place in the Charlie Hall Chase at Wetherby. "Colin Tizzard and all the team at home had him in some

"

If I'd dreamed 1,000 times I'd never have thought I would be lucky enough to ride a horse like him"

PADDY BRENNAN

Paddy Brennan with Daisy Burton, Bob and Jean Bishop's great-granddaughter

form. I hacked him to the start and I knew instantly things were going to be so much different today," said Brennan.

"He was the Cue Card I know. When he's in that form you can ride him whatever way you want, he's different class.

"I'm lucky to be riding him and he keeps surprising me how good he is; when he has the right conditions with a little bit of ease underfoot it's dangerous what he can do. If I'd dreamed 1,000 times I'd never have thought I would be lucky enough to ride a horse like him."

HAYDOCK
Betfair Chase

2014–15   2015–16   2016–17   2017–18

MAR | APR | NOV | DEC | JAN | FEB | MAR | APR | NOV | DEC | JAN | FEB | MAR | APR | NOV | DEC | JAN | FEB | MAR | APR

"

I'm not saying he's
Kauto Star but he's
got an aura, he's got
a following of so
many people"

PADDY BRENNAN

Lucky to be on him, perhaps, but riding a successful chaser – who has claims to be the most popular horse in training – brings its own pressures.

"There is a responsibility in riding a horse like Cue Card," Brennan said. "I'm not saying he's Kauto Star but he's got an aura, he's got a following of so many people.

"I felt a lot of pressure today. I felt maybe it got away in the Gold Cup last year but after today I think we've got a chance of putting that right.

"This was always in the back of my mind after I reached 1,000; there was never going to be much celebration until after I rode Cue Card today. I've got no rides tomorrow, so there will be celebrations."

Those celebrations were more than justified. However, in racing you are barely allowed to celebrate a success before questions of the next mission are raised. The next mission for Cue Card was obvious – Kempton, the King George and a first showdown with Thistlecrack.

The sport's most exciting young talent had contested three novice chases and won all three, easily and by wide margins. Save for a couple of hairy moments at a Cheltenham open ditch, he had jumped with aplomb. He was also soon to become a nine-year-old, which influenced Tizzard and owners John and Heather Snook into accelerating the former outstanding hurdler's chasing progress.

There was no danger of a jockey clash. Thistlecrack was very much the mount of Tom Scudamore, who was not surprisingly confident. So, too, though, was Brennan, who said: "If Cue Card runs up to his best and Thistlecrack still beats us, I will never have ridden against, or seen, a better horse. I genuinely believe that. If we're beaten then so be it, but I'll be going out there thinking I'm on the best horse and not expecting defeat."

On this occasion, however, Brennan was defeated. Thistlecrack edged out Cue Card for favouritism – the novice was returned 11-10 with his teammate on 5-4 – and he proved too good in the race, helped by Cue Card running a full stone below his Betfair Chase-winning form.

Thistlecrack justified owners John and Heather Snook's bold decision to pitch their novice into the big time as he produced a prodigious round of jumping and galloping to become the first novice to win the Grade 1 Boxing Day feature.

Stablemate and last year's King George winner Cue Card was brushed aside by the home turn as Thistlecrack seemingly effortlessly maintained his gallop as his four rivals flagged.

Tom Scudamore, never feeling the need to pick up his whip, nudged Thistlecrack fully eight lengths clear before having the luxury of looking round on the run-in to tell his eight-year-old partner he had done more than enough.

Cue Card and Hamir Singh (far side) work with Theatre Guide and Kim Tizzard at Venn Farm stables in November 2016

HAYDOCK
Betfair Chase

KEMPTON
32Red King George VI Chase

2014-15   2015-16   2016-17   2017-18

MAR | APR | NOV | DEC | JAN | FEB | MAR | APR | NOV | DEC | JAN | FEB | MAR | APR | NOV | DEC | JAN | FEB | MAR | APR | NOV | DEC | JAN | FEB | MAR | APR

Colin Tizzard, whose one-two in the race took him past £1 million in prize-money for the season, looked the coolest man on the track. "You should put your hand on my heart," said the Dorset trainer. "That's the most nerve-wracking thing I've ever watched, especially when they came together like that from a fair way out.

"I thought, 'here we go', but in the end it was lovely, a fantastic performance by both horses. They've done very well – they're good boys."

Paddy Brennan asked Cue Card to give Thistlecrack something to think about down the back straight, but his challenge foundered on the rock that is Thistlecrack, who was still swinging along in Scudamore's hands as the other four were flat out into the home bend.

The acclaim had started as Scudamore corrected him to shorten into the last before popping over safely and being eased on the run-in to win by three and a quarter lengths.

Cue Card gamely held second from Silviniaco Conti, who had dropped back to a detached last of the five on the home turn but stayed on to nearly snatch second.

Paddy Brennan tried everything on Cue Card to put Thistlecrack under pressure but the pair were toiling on the final bend.

"He gave his all," said Brennan. "The ground always felt on the quicker side, a bit like Wetherby. I was never that happy, but take nothing away from the winner.

"I wasn't travelling as well as I'd like to but Thistlecrack does things with such ease. He reminds me of the greats, like Denman and Kauto Star. I'm really proud of Cue Card though." (Bruce Jackson)

As the dust settled on the King George, Colin Tizzard began to wonder if the Gold Cup should this time be Cue Card's festival aim, his thinking influenced by having not only Thistlecrack for the Gold Cup, but also Native River, who had enjoyed a stunning winter, winning two of the sport's hottest handicaps, the Hennessy Gold Cup and Coral Welsh Grand National.

"

That's the most nerve-wracking thing I've ever watched, especially when they came together like that from a fair way out"

COLIN TIZZARD

2009-10   2010-11   2011-12   2012-13   2013-14

JAN | FEB | MAR | APR | NOV | DEC | JAN | FEB | MAR | APR | NOV | DEC | JAN | FEB | MAR | APR | NOV | DEC | JAN | FEB | MAR | APR | NOV | DEC | JAN | FEB

"We're definitely thinking of the Ryanair," said Tizzard. "It's up to the owners but I might send Cue Card to the Ascot Chase and the Ryanair Chase because I don't really want Native River, Cue Card and Thistlecrack in the same race. I want to protect Cue Card.

"Cue Card paid the penalty a bit for chasing Thistlecrack in the country. It was good for him to hang on to second."

They thought long and hard about it. They knew Cue Card was favourite for the Ryanair but also knew they wanted to win the Gold Cup more. Therefore, even before Cue Card ran in the Betfair Ascot

Paddy Brennan (right) on Cue Card congratulates Tom Scudamore after the latter's King George victory on Thistlecrack at Kempton in December 2016

KEMPTON
32Red King George VI Chase

2014–15   2015–16   2016–17   2017–18
MAR APR NOV DEC JAN FEB MAR APR NOV DEC JAN FEB MAR APR NOV DEC JAN FEB MAR APR NOV DEC JAN FEB MAR APR

"
He jumped fantastic
and destroyed them.
It was everything I
could have wanted
and more"

COLIN TIZZARD

3.35　Betfair Ascot Chase (Grade
[OFF 3.38]　**1) Class 1**　　17 fences(2m5f8y) 2m5f
For: 5-y-o and up 1st £85,425 2nd £32,055 3rd £16,050 4th £7,995 5th £4,020 6th
£2,010
1　**CUE CARD** 11 11-7 t ....(170) **Paddy Brennan**
　 b g by King's Theatre (IRE)–Wicked Crack (IRE) (King's Ride
　 (IRE)
　 (Colin Tizzard) tracked leader, challenged 4 out, led next, easily
　 drew right away from 2 out　　　　　　　[op 1/2] 4/9F
2　15**SHANTOU FLYER (IRE)** 7 11-7 t .....(156) Adam Wedge
　 b g by Shantou (USA)–Carrigmorna Flyer (IRE) (Bob Back (USA))
　 (Rebecca Curtis) chased leading pair to 9th, outpaced from 13th,
　 went 3rd again after 3 out, kept on to take remote 2nd after last
　　　　　　　　　　　　　[op 20/1 tchd 25/1] 22/1
3　3¾ ROYAL REGATTA (IRE) 9 11-7 tb (157) Richard Johnson
　[18¾] b g by King's Theatre (IRE)–Friendly Craic (IRE) (Mister Lord
　 (USA))
　 (Philip Hobbs) led, stretched on from 10th, pressed 4 out, headed
　 next but well clear of rest, tried to fight back but beaten when
　 mistake 2 out, weakened and lost 2nd after last
　　　　　　　　　　　　　 [op 9/1 tchd 12/1] 11/1

Opposite: Paddy Brennan drives Cue Card
to a popular victory in the Ascot Chase in
February 2017

Chase, Jean Bishop had stated her star's festival aim would be the Gold Cup. First, there was the little matter of the Ascot Chase, a race Cue Card had won four years earlier under Joe Tizzard. He would win it again under Paddy Brennan.

His younger stablemates may have stolen the limelight in recent months, but at Ascot, Cue Card served a timely reminder of his own wondrous talent.

It would be even-money each of two as to which was more electric – the 11-year-old's open display of authority or the reception he received upon his return to the winner's enclosure.

The race between scrambling fans clamouring for a vantage point from which to greet their hero was vastly more competitive than the Grade 1 Cue Card had just made a mockery of, winning by an eased-down 15 lengths under a broad-grinning Paddy Brennan.

It was a welcome that touched all connected with this most majestic horse.

In Thistlecrack and Native River, Colin Tizzard may have two horses deemed by bookmakers to have a better chance of winning next month's Gold Cup, but the trainer knows Cue Card – a general 6-1 chance for the Cheltenham showpiece – is the most popular.

"He's such a superstar," Tizzard said. "He's surprised me all my life, he's been a brilliant horse for such a long time and deserved that reception.

"You keep worrying as he's 11 and you wonder can he keep doing this? I've been doing this with him for years and he was brilliant again today. He jumped fantastic and destroyed them. It was everything I could have wanted and more."

A disappointing second in the King George had raised questions as to whether Father Time was beginning to catch up with him, but his trainer had a different explanation.

He said: "After his last race he wasn't right behind, he had a big fat leg afterwards. He had a bit of lymphangitis – he didn't have it when he raced but you don't know if it affected him."

ASCOT
Betfair Ascot Chase

Paddy Brennan acknowledges the cheers of the crowd as he returns on Ascot Chase hero Cue Card

Once that cleared up, Tizzard, who suggested despite the growing strength of his team that he still did not have a horse who could beat Cue Card up his four-furlong gallop, was talked into a detour from last year's path by Cue Card's jockey.

"Paddy was the instigator of this," explained Tizzard. "He said to come here because over two and a half they'd go a Cheltenham pace, we wouldn't have to have three months off and it would fire him up and keep his jumping sharp."

Brennan may have been in the saddle for only ten of Cue Card's 35 career starts, but his deep love for the horse is obvious.

He has won a World Hurdle and a Gold Cup, but he had also endured a meandering few years and when he said "he's changed my life in the last couple of years" he was not joking.

"He's a serious machine," was his glowing appraisal of Cue Card's ninth Grade 1 win and his second Ascot Chase four years after his first. "I was most impressed from the second-last to the last, he picked up like a good horse should."

Of the Gold Cup, he added: "In a normal year he'd be a short-priced favourite, but this is an exceptional Gold Cup. It's going to be an unbelievable race but he'll be ridden different tactically and if they get into it a long way out it could just fall in his lap.

"I certainly wouldn't swap him for either of the other two and I'm sure he won't let us down." (Stuart Riley)

Brennan's devotion to Cue Card had deepened again. Alastair Down felt the same.

They came, they saw, he conquered. Four years on from his last victory in the Ascot Chase, Cue Card purred home to win by 15 lengths – a beautifully tuned V8 making his rivals look like two-stroke lawnmowers.

It is the four-year gap that tells you so much about this horse, a household god in many a jumping dwelling.

Cue Card has been at it for a long time now and has built up a mighty back catalogue of greatest hits. He is becoming a bit like Frank Sinatra on tour, and back in November on Betfair Chase day at Haydock he might have said to the crowd, "You've seen me do this race a couple of times before, in '13 and '15, well, here's my 2016 rearrangement."

And of course Cue Card's faithful fans love the show and the performer who first topped the bill as a 40-1 chance when slamming Al Ferof by eight lengths in the Champion Bumper in 2010, when pterodactyls still wheeled high over Cleeve Hill.

Seven years on he is still going strong, and that is an achievement in itself. He is a steeplechaser not a florist, and his place of work has been all coalface.

He has covered more than 80 miles pitched in uniformly jumped countless obstacles, plus stood a training regime that isn't for softies.

Colin Tizzard does not send his horses out to race with a bit left to work on – they get a tough prep for hard races.

In terms of soundness alone, Cue Card is a marvel. Just think how many times those tendons have hammered down

> **"**
> He's a serious machine"
> **PADDY BRENNAN**

ASCOT
Betfair Ascot Chase

2014–15   2015–16   2016–17   2017–18

MAR   APR   NOV   DEC   JAN   FEB   MAR   APR   NOV   DEC   JAN   FEB   MAR   APR   NOV   DEC   JAN   FEB   MAR   APR   NOV   DEC   JAN   FEB   MAR   APR

and been stretched. Greybeards don't talk about 'if' a horse gets a leg but 'when'. The physical strains are enormous, but Cue Card has so far ploughed his furrow seemingly immune to the attritional wear and tear.

If he were a soldier he wouldn't be in the catering corps, you would find him in the commandos or with the SAS flogging across the Brecon Beacons, which is probably the one place Tizzard has yet to gallop him.

Small wonder the public have cleaved to him in such a way. In 35 races he has unseated once and fallen once – and it is that fall so many of his fans ache to see avenged next month.

We are a sentimental lot and there was something of the gods getting in a grump and ganging up on him in last year's Gold Cup.

Cue Card was still travelling first-class in the wide-ass seats when falling three out and the groan that greeted his departure must have echoed all the way down past the Severn Bridge.

After yesterday's win, Paddy Brennan, who always had Cue Card handy in second, said: "He's going to be ridden radically differently in the Gold Cup and if they get into a fight a long way out it could just fall into his lap."

It must surely be the case that the Tizzard family have never clapped eyes on a horse they loved more than Cue Card.

Yet here is the old man, Colin, conspiring with malice aforethought to poop the party with the two horses ahead of him in the Gold Cup market, Thistlecrack and Native River.

Cue Card must have every right to mumble away in his box to the effect: "I graft season in and season out, making a fortune for this farm that wouldn't have seen a new tractor in years without me, and what gratitude do I get? The old so-and-so comes up with not one but two who could do the proverbial on my chips on Gold Cup day."

Although racing has an endless capacity for fairy tales at the festival, it takes a leap of faith to see Cue Card righting last year's wrong. But the beauty of chasers like him is that you can rule nothing out.

His greatest fan was at Ascot in the still spry form of owner Jean Bishop. It must still be a wonderful experience to greet her old stalwart back to the winner's enclosure, although doubtless not a patch on the days when her husband Bob, a man of many qualities, stood towering over her alongside.

Cue Card for the Gold Cup? Cheltenham is taking no chances and the huge bolts holding the roof on are due an extra tightening this week.

Cue Card looks a picture with groom Hamir Singh at Colin Tizzard's yard in February 2017 as the trainer prepared his star for a second tilt at the Cheltenham Gold Cup

ASCOT
Betfair Ascot Chase

The roof would not be raised for Thistlecrack. A tendon injury ruled him out of the Gold Cup, leaving Tizzard to chase Gold Cup laurels with Cue Card – who, at 11, was seeking to become the first horse older than ten to win since 1969 – and Native River.

In the Racing Post's Gold Cup preview, he confessed he had never known a feeling to match the time when his son drove Cue Card home in front seven years earlier.

"When Joe rode him here in the Champion Bumper, I've never experienced that type of emotion before or since, and he's kept on doing it for seven seasons," he said.

"We did miss two festivals with him, so we've had downers, but they were only little problems, right before the festival, and luckily he's been good enough to come through them.

"I'd just love to do it for the horse. We had it in our mind last year was perhaps his chance, as a ten-year-old, and maybe he wouldn't be as good this year, but he's come out as good as he ever was."

Asked about what happened at the third-last fence 12 months earlier, he added: "The Cheltenham Gold Cup is a very big strain on an owner, trainer, horse and jockey. I'm sure if Paddy had his time again he wouldn't be where he was at that time, but if you look four fences earlier Cue Card was off the bridle not going anywhere, then a gap opened and he took off.

"None of us ever thought he'd fall as he's always been a very neat and accurate jumper. It was a horrible fall and I was just glad to see him get up, but Paddy took it that he was in the wrong place at the wrong time. There's nothing wrong with that and I don't want to wind Paddy up about it – he's wound up enough!"

From the Cheltenham press room late on Gold Cup afternoon I found myself writing that Brennan had been left with reason to feel wound up again.

The third-last fence on Cheltenham's New course is set to be forever associated with Cue Card, but for all the wrong reasons, after the most popular horse in training once again crashed out of the Gold Cup at his birch-packed nemesis.

Twelve months ago there was agony for the star's connec-

tions and fans when he fell while still cruising and with a £1 million bonus in sight, causing jockey Paddy Brennan to subsequently admit: "I wanted to die."

Cue Card jumps in unison with Tea For Two in the Betway Bowl at Aintree in April 2017 before going on to finish second to that rival

At the very same fence, and in a miserably similar way, the 11-year-old fell once again, barely picking up and paying the price. This time he was being pushed along having travelled with little fluency down the back straight.

To everyone's relief, Cue Card galloped away from the scene of the accident – and he is set to carry on galloping in races.

Owner Jean Bishop had suggested her veteran would be retired if victorious. Given the very different outcome, a trip to Aintree – where he was so imperious last year – could now beckon.

Asked if Cue Card would carry on racing, trainer Colin Tizzard said: "I should think so. Why not? There's not a scratch on him."

CHELTENHAM
Timico Cheltenham
Gold Cup Chase

2014-15   2015-16   2016-17   2017-18

MAR | APR | NOV | DEC | JAN | FEB | MAR | APR | NOV | DEC | JAN | FEB | MAR | APR | NOV | DEC | JAN | FEB | MAR | APR | NOV | DEC | JAN | FEB | MAR | APR

Tizzard's son Joe – Cue Card's rider for his two festival wins – added: "If he comes out of this okay we'll probably go to Aintree. There are certainly no plans to retire him. He fell too far out today to say he was beaten, but Paddy was niggling him and he definitely wasn't travelling as well as he had been last year. That's the way he races now."

Over the following days, the Tizzards more than once repeated that there were no plans to retire Cue Card. True to their word, they ran him at Aintree in the race he had landed with such elan the previous April. This time he had to settle for second best, denied by Tea For Two in a driving finish.

Better, however, to finish the season with an admirable second than a crashing fall.

David Carr was the Racing Post's Betway Bowl reporter.

He seems to have been around forever, he is renowned for the way he bounces back from adversity and his recent fall has clearly not got the better of him.

Ken Barlow may still be recuperating in *Coronation Street*, but across the ITV schedule Cue Card showed there is still plenty of active life in him.

He had fallen three out in the Gold Cup for the second year in a row, and while he may well have been an unlucky loser at Cheltenham in 2016 he'd not looked to be going well 12 months on.

Yet this is a chaser who has made a career out of returning from disappointment. Twice already this season he had come back from a below-form effort to score in Grade 1 company.

He threatened to make it a treble for much of the way in the Betway Bowl under an attacking ride by Paddy Brennan, and Colin Tizzard was far from upset with his neck defeat.

"It was a fantastic run," the trainer said. "He loved being ridden that positive. The front two were very close in the King George and very close today, and the third horse was 15 lengths behind."

Tizzard added there are no plans for imminent retirement.

"I know people are saying he's 11 but he's as good as he's ever been and loves racing like that. He can go out in the field and come back next season.

"He's still got plenty of pace and was outstayed by a real stayer. It doesn't have to be the Gold Cup, it could be the Ryanair. I'm not saying he won't go to the Gold Cup, but there are plenty of other races he can do as well."

Much of what Tizzard suggested at Aintree might happen in the season that followed duly did happen. Unfortunately, the season started with something they very much did not want to happen.

At home, Cue Card was reported by Tizzard to be "burning up our gallops" and sparkling in advance of starting his ninth season on the track. The first stop on the road was again Wetherby for the Charlie Hall Chase, a contest in which he was travelling generously when crashing out at the final fence down the back straight, five from home.

He did, however, have a genuine excuse, as David Carr noted.

Next time someone complains about fences being omitted owing to the low sun, remind them of the 2017 bet365 Charlie Hall Chase.

When somebody says it's 'health and safety gone mad', tell them of the day the blinding effects of the light may have stopped the two market leaders even getting round.

Neither Coneygree nor Cue Card, both experienced and top-class chasers, completed the course – and the finger of blame was pointed at the low-lying sun in both cases.

Coneygree, the 2015 Cheltenham Gold Cup winner, took off much too early at the first ditch, the third fence overall, which is halfway down the back straight.

That is reckoned to have unnerved him as he lost his confidence and he was pulled up by Nico de Boinville with a circuit to go.

Cue Card fell at the last fence in the back straight on the final circuit, five from home, and again the low sun was blamed.

> He can go out in the field and come back next season"
>
> **COLIN TIZZARD**

CHELTENHAM
Timico Cheltenham
Gold Cup Chase

AINTREE
Betway Bowl
Chase

WETHERBY
bet365 Charlie
Hall Chase

2014–15   2015–16   2016–17   2017–18

MAR APR NOV DEC JAN FEB MAR APR NOV DEC JAN FEB MAR APR NOV DEC JAN FEB MAR APR

Previous spread: Harry Cobden and Cue Card
parade before the Betfair Chase at Haydock
in November 2017. The pair finished a distant
second to Bristol De Mai

"He took his eye off it," said jockey Paddy Brennan. "Early on in the race he was a bit sluggish but once I got him up there down the back I was happier.

"But fallers don't win races. He was all right and there's always another day."

On four previous occasions that day had been in mid-November at Haydock. Cue Card had won the Betfair Chase on three occasions, only one less than the mighty Kauto Star. It was the obvious place for him to go. He went.

But he went with another jockey on his back.

Paddy Brennan had been the chosen one for Cue Card's last 13 races. Two of those last three races had ended in a heavy fall. A new pair of hands was deemed worth trying, so the team selected teenage sensation Harry Cobden, by that point already established as a key member of Paul Nicholls' riding squad.

"I like the idea of having a younger man on him," said Tizzard, adding: "It is fresh hands on board so we will see what happens."

What happened was not particularly nice to see, although Cobden could hardly be blamed.

Cue Card was strongly fancied by many to win. Bristol De Mai, who had survived the sun to score at Wetherby, was the race's 11-10 favourite, his position at the head of the betting in part due to him being proven on the heavy ground that Haydock was offering. There are few things so heavy as Haydock heavy. On this particular afternoon, Haydock was very heavy indeed. Bristol De Mai was almost certain to love it. He showed he loved it with a rare passion. Cue Card did not.

On his first outing under Cobden, Cue Card finished second. The problem was he finished 57 lengths behind Bristol De Mai. The attributed Racing Post Rating for his performance of 125 was lower than for any of his completed starts, save for his debut in the Fontwell bumper.

The margin between the first two home in the Betfair Chase was a staggering 57 lengths, but perhaps the most telling number was five.

> "
> I like the idea of having a younger man on him. It is fresh hands on board, so we will see what happens"
>
> **COLIN TIZZARD**

That is the difference in years between Bristol De Mai, who despite seeming like he has been around forever is only six, and 11-year-old Cue Card, who was made to look his age by a horse thriving in his optimum conditions.

Having hit the deck twice on his last three starts, Cue Card had questions to answer as he went in search of emulating Kauto Star's four victories in the Grade 1 contest.

However, despite the youthful exuberance of his new 19-year-old jockey Harry Cobden, taking over from Paddy Brennan, the Colin Tizzard-trained fans' favourite could not match Kauto Star after running in snatches before finishing tired.

"He was second to a very good horse, who has blown the race away from start to finish," said Tizzard.

"He doesn't swing on the bridle like he used to but that's why he stays well. In previous years it has been sloshy ground here and he never really travelled today on that holding ground and, in the end, he's finished tired."

The retirement talk from some quarters, which followed his comeback fall in the Charlie Hall Chase, is only likely to intensify, but Tizzard was holding fire on the future.

"They're not machines and we've just run into a good one, and he still had enough to finish second," said the trainer. "He jumped around clear and we'll go away and make plans."

Cue Card was pushed out to a high of 40-1 for next month's 32Red King George VI Chase, a race he won in 2015 and finished second in last year. (Andrew Dietz)

When a treasured old horse runs badly, there are inevitably calls for that horse to be retired. In the era of social media, those calls are louder than they would have been in the past. The calls for Cue Card to be retired were by now easy to hear.

Those who know him best, and loved him most, felt differently. Horses constantly bounce back from seemingly dismal showings. They are not machines. If they have good days, the majority will also have the odd bad day.

> "
> He jumped around clear and we'll go away and make plans"
>
> **COLIN TIZZARD**

WETHERBY
bet365 Charlie Hall Chase

HAYDOCK
Betfair Chase

| 2014-15 | | | | | | | 2015-16 | | | | | | | 2016-17 | | | | | | | 2017-18 | | | | |
| MAR | APR | NOV | DEC | JAN | FEB | MAR | APR | NOV | DEC | JAN | FEB | MAR | APR | NOV | DEC | JAN | FEB | MAR | APR | NOV | DEC | JAN | FEB | MAR | APR |

"

Win, lose or draw, it is a delight as well as a privilege to be getting on the old boy again"

PADDY BRENNAN

At the same time, the Bishop and Tizzard families recognised Cue Card was on the back nine and, in racing terms, walking ever closer to the clubhouse. They acknowledged this would almost certainly be his final campaign and that where he ran had to be thought about long and hard.

They thought about the King George but decided against it. They then thought about a Listed chase at Kempton's following meeting in early January. He might well have gone there but for being briefly sidelined with pus in a foot.

It was eventually decided Cue Card's 40th race would be in one he had won twice before, the Betfair Ascot Chase. He was returning to a place he knew well. He would again be ridden by a jockey he knew well. Brennan was back on his back.

Cobden had been called up by Nicholls to work at Wincanton. That meant Cue Card was without a rider. Not, however, for long.

"I know there were a few names in the hat to ride him this weekend but I think it speaks volumes about Colin Tizzard that he has put me back on the horse after taking me off," said Brennan.

"Not many owners and trainers have done that before with me and it shows the people that Jean and Colin are.

"Win, lose or draw, it is a delight as well as a privilege to be getting on the old boy again. I love him to bits, whatever happens on Saturday."

We were reminded of the wider love for Cue Card by the reaction to his Ascot exertions. He did not win but he ran the most wonderful race, this time without his customary noseband. Leading from the off at high speed and jumping with a zest that showed how much he still loved his job, he repelled everything except the tremendously exciting Waiting Patiently, an opponent five years his junior.

I was there for the Racing Post and, hand on heart, can say I have seldom enjoyed watching a horse lose more. His effort in defeat stirred the soul.

He lost, but it did not feel like that.

As soon as Cue Card passed the winning line, racegoers moved at speeds to which they are almost certainly not accustomed, sprinting to reach the rail along the walkway. Once there, they applauded him off the racecourse and then, as he entered the paddock in the most glorious defeat, a different group of fans made the sort of noise that greets very few Ascot winners.

It was all rather wonderful.

So, too, of course, is Cue Card. When we last saw jumping's most popular performer, he was clambering over Haydock's final fence en route to a 57-length defeat. Before that he had suffered a horrible fall at Wetherby, only two runs after his second Cheltenham Gold Cup crash. On his return to a familiar stage we feared for him, but only because we love him. Now both our affection and admiration for Cue Card is deeper than ever.

In his attempt to win a third Betfair Ascot Chase, in which all Cue Card's rivals were upwards of four years his junior, Colin Tizzard took the sheepskin noseband off and put Paddy Brennan back on.

Brennan, on board for five of Cue Card's nine Grade 1s, ignited his old friend from flagfall and asked him one overriding question. He demanded to know if the spark was still there. What he felt and what we saw is that it is.

Jean Bishop's pride and joy appeared to love every second of his afternoon at Ascot, racing with a relish and glee that was a joy to watch. It settled your nerves and allowed you to enjoy what was to come.

On the second climb from Swinley Bottom, the dual Cheltenham Festival winner positively soared over the uphill fences, and even when headed by Waiting Patiently, the fight was plainly still in his belly.

At the age of 12, Cue Card has made a comeback.

"That was probably one of the best rides I've had off him – he never gives up," said Brennan, who can now look forward to Cheltenham, where the veteran could bid to regain the Ryanair Chase he captured in 2013 or seek Gold Cup redemption, having fallen three out the last two seasons.

ASCOT
Betfair Ascot Chase

Cue Card (left) is denied by Waiting Patiently after a thrilling run in the Ascot Chase in February 2018

"He was brilliant all the way round," said Tizzard.

"Goodness me, he has been that good at home, but I'm so glad he's done it here. He's just a good boy.

"He'll go to Cheltenham, but it's no good asking me which race. There is unfinished business in one race and he has won the other before.

Ultimately it will be Jean's choice.

"The feeling is mainly relief. There's pressure training horses, there's no two ways about that. If you don't feel pressure you probably shouldn't be training. If you do feel pressure you probably shouldn't be training, either. This horse is a pleasure to train though."

Explaining why there had been a headgear change, Tizzard added: "We've had him for nine seasons now. Sometimes you have to change things in life a bit. He had a noseband on because he holds his head up a little, but we never ride him in one at home. We schooled him in a grackle bridle on Thursday and Paddy had a job to hold him. We could see he was enjoying it, so we decided to let him run loose."

"He ran like a horse let loose, full of the zest that hallmarked his Champion Bumper triumph all those years ago."

Bishop's reply, asked how she felt watching the race, was: "Don't ask me!"

Yet she surely felt better after than she had before. We all did. The wonderful Cue Card story continues.

We all now expected it to continue at Cheltenham, and it did, but in the Ryanair Chase not the Gold Cup. Both races were weighed up, but with the Ryanair looking to be clearly the easier option it was announced that would be his target.

Sadly, this would not be the perfect festival farewell.

> **"**
> He ran like a horse
> let loose, full of the
> zest that hallmarked
> his Champion Bumper
> triumph all those
> years ago"
>
> **COLIN TIZZARD**

Colin Tizzard at home with Cue Card in February 2018

ASCOT
Betfair Ascot
Chase

CHELTENHAM
Ryanair Chase

Cue Card and Paddy Brennan make their way back after pulling up in the Ryanair Chase at the 2018 Cheltenham Festival in what turned out to be his final race

It started well, with Cue Card leading over the early fences, but not long after the lead was lost it was obvious the old boy was struggling to remain in contention on ground far softer than is usually seen at Cheltenham in March.

Brennan did the sensible thing and took Cue Card out of the race, pulling him up before the 12th fence. To watch that happen was an odd experience, for while it was deflating, there was also a degree of relief. Moreover, this was still an opportunity to say thank you, which countless racegoers did, heartily applauding their veteran friend off the racecourse, up the horsewalk and then back to the area where unplaced horses are unsaddled.

"It was the last thing I expected," said Tizzard of the performance.

"Paddy said he was never travelling on that deep ground and when they went by him he couldn't handle it. Paddy had to make a split decision. He was in last place and there was no use carrying on. It was sad to see him stop so quickly. But he's walking around bright as a button after the race."

On the subject of retirement he said: "We're not going to mention that word – but it's getting closer."

It was closer than we had been led to think.

Jean Bishop revealed Cue Card would have what she called his 'retirement race' in the Oaksey Chase on the season's final day at Sandown. It was a contest that looked potentially ideal but everyone associated with the horse had always stressed he would only run if firing on all cylinders at home. It became clear he was not. On the morning of April 17, 2018, Cue Card's retirement was announced.

"In the end he wasn't showing the sparkle he'd shown," said Tizzard.

"It was a lovely decision to make. It's a weight off my mind. It would have been too big a call to race him again. He cantered this morning and jumped. He has been a fantastic horse all the way round, and he is fit and sound, but I kept looking at him and thought this is not the Cue Card we know.

"He had a hard race the other day and in any other year we would have turned him out and had him in next season. It's a lovely time to retire him."

The £1,447,454 accumulated by Cue Card since his 41-race career began in January 2010 placed him in the top ten in terms of prize-money won by jumpers trained in Europe. A large chunk of that money was earned in the hands of Paddy Brennan, who passed on his own heartfelt words, while also honestly casting his mind back to that infamous 2016 Gold Cup fall.

"It was my lowest moment as a jockey," he said. "He was the best horse I have ridden not to win a Gold Cup. I was just as gutted for his owners and connections as myself. I just wanted to disappear."

Brennan added: "The thing that separated this horse from the rest, aside from his longevity, was his ability to bounce back, and to do so in a very short space of time. He went to Aintree less than three weeks after that Cheltenham fall and destroyed Don Poli in the Bowl. That was another hallmark of the horse – his ability to prove the doubters wrong.

"Yes, there were plenty of disappointments along the way, but

> **"**
> It's a lovely time
> to retire him"
> **COLIN TIZZARD**

CHELTENHAM
Ryanair Chase

When he was born
I couldn't believe
my luck"
ROWLAND CRELLIN

you will take those all day long when you look at what success and joy he gave to me and others.

"It was a privilege to be associated with such a legend of a horse, one I genuinely love to bits."

Brennan made a point of thanking Bob Bishop and his widow Jean for giving him the opportunity to forge a relationship with a thoroughbred whose owner was first and foremost delighted her star was bowing out healthy, happy and still able to parade at Sandown, where thousands of fans were able to say goodbye.

"It is the end of an era," said Jean. "I feel quite sad about it but all good things come to an end. We knew it was imminent but happening like it did was unexpected."

On a day of tributes, another came from Cue Card's breeder, Rowland Crellin. "When he was born I couldn't believe my luck," he said, describing the then foal as "beautifully correct, quick to learn and trouble-free".

That was how he started. He finished as the nation's favourite racehorse, one well worthy of a final curtain-falling piece from Alastair Down.

It took the ancient chroniclers around 260 chapters to knock out the story of Jesus and his mates in the New Testament, so how do you shoehorn the incarnation of Cue Card into 600 words?

Of course Jesus performed his miracles – raising Lazarus from the dead always a touch less impressive than the water into wine trick at Cana – but the son of God never won the King George, let alone three Betfair Chases.

And in an increasingly secular Britain, it is likely that among Racing Post readers, Cue Card could probably muster more followers than the man from Nazareth.

Both spent time in the wilderness. A mere 40 days back in biblical times whereas the redoubtable Cue Card spent the entire 2014–15 season in a winless desert before rising again to reclaim former glories and go on to achieve mightier feats.

What was extraordinary about Cue Card was the happy grip

he exerted on the racing public and the way in which he came to be carried along on a rising tide of popularity and surge of unvarnished affection.

He acquired the status of most popular chaser in training and that is a gift not lightly earned. Jumps fans are a sentimental bunch – it is one of the ties that bind – but we don't dispense our admiration willy-nilly.

Like trust it has to be earned, and in the case of the staying chaser, hard earned. We need to see them going through the mill season in season out before the scales fall from our eyes and there is suddenly mass accord that we are in the presence of the unforgettable.

And we are suckers for triumph over adversity. That is how it should be – in racing as in life.

That is why Cue Card's victory on November 21 in the 2015 Betfair Chase was such a milestone.

He had warmed up for Haydock by winning his first race for 23 months with a favoured-by-the-weights success in the Charlie Hall. But the Betfair was an altogether more acid test. Could he still cut the mustard at the top level?

Cut it? He lacerated it, winning all but on the bridle from old rival Silviniaco Conti. He was not only back but firing broadsides – it was akin to the restoration of the monarchy.

And it was the first time we truly understood what he meant to the benign toughie that is Colin Tizzard. It was Cue Card who gave us Tizzard the trainer rather than the farmer, whizzing him up in the express lift from middle storeys to the penthouse suite.

Tizzard stood there in the winner's enclosure trying to blink back tears. The score was Ducts 1 – Dorset 0. And quite right too.

But while those who love Cue Card have been to plenty of wonderful weddings, there have been memorial services as well. Agonising Gold Cup falls ensuring that Cue Card is doomed ever to wander that tantalising unmapped country of the might have been.

> **"**
> He acquired the status of most popular chaser in training and that is a gift not lightly earned"
>
> **ALASTAIR DOWN**

2014-15   2015-16   2016-17   2017-18

MAR | APR | NOV | DEC | JAN | FEB | MAR | APR | NOV | DEC | JAN | FEB | MAR | APR | NOV | DEC | JAN | FEB | MAR | APR | NOV | DEC | JAN | FEB | MAR | APR

On his racecourse debut in January 2010 he bolted up in a bumper at Fontwell. A happy Colin Tizzard pottered down to the winner's enclosure but of son Joe and the winner there was no sign.

The wait stretched into minutes. Still no horse. Truth be told Joe simply could not pull him up.

It is seven miles from Fontwell to Goodwood and they say Trundle Hill did the trick.

Beautifully served by connections, he has been taking us all over happy horizons ever since.

Now he returns to Hardy country and hardy is exactly what he has been. The chaser as chum. And we rightly grow very attached to them.

Opposite: Cue Card paraded in front of
thousands of fans at Sandown on the final
day of the 2017–18 jumps season

APPRECIATION
Lee Mottershead

Those who love jump racing will always be grateful to Cue Card. The gratitude felt by those people lucky enough to have been most closely associated with him is immeasurable.

To Colin Tizzard, he was the animal whose rise to racing stardom helped power his own. He would be the first to admit as much, just as Joe Tizzard would tell you the raw young athlete he could barely control in that debut Fontwell bumper subsequently gave him the sort of glory afternoons he must have thought by then had become improbable. He revived his first rider's career and then did the same for Paddy Brennan.

To the Tizzards and Brennan, Cue Card was a very special friend. To Jean Bishop and her children he was even more than that. He became a living extension of the husband and father they said a sudden goodbye to only four days after that monumental triumph in the 2015 King George VI Chase.

Bob Bishop adored Cue Card. So did – and so do – his family. By racing on after Bob's death, Cue Card kept the memory of an old-fashioned patriarch going. Now he will race no longer, but the memories they have of the man and his horse, often when sharing the same stage, are set to be of enormous comfort as they come to terms with deep loss.

"I used to think all the time Cue Card was racing that nothing would happen with Dad," says Bob's daughter Lesley Bourne.

"I always said Cue Card kept him alive. He used to love seeing him race so much. He had lots of health scares and health issues over the Cue Card years but he would never not go to one of the races.

"Now that Cue Card won't be racing any more it's going to make it seem even more real that Dad isn't here. The horse has definitely helped us cope with losing him."

It is a mark of Cue Card's tremendous longevity that the majority of his major victories came when Bob was still alive. He was an omnipresent of the jumps scene, a horse who had already secured the first of what would be nine Grade 1 triumphs many months before Frankel had even set foot on a racecourse. The last two top-flight successes came after members of Frankel's first crop of racehorses had already started winning.

Gordon Brown was still prime minister when Cue Card, a 40-1 shot unconsidered by most punters, romped to victory in the 2010 Champion Bumper. I was one of those who had been hugely impressed by his tour de force at Fontwell, but I gave him no financial support at Cheltenham, the reason being it was hard to imagine Colin Tizzard training a Champion Bumper winner.

Back then it was. Now it is not. One day after Cue Card raced for the final time his stable companion Native River captured the Gold Cup. Tizzard had risen to the peak of his profession. It was the completion of a journey that was given priceless impetus as dusk descended on Cheltenham during that Champion Bumper evening. For the Tizzard family's racing business, Cue Card was a calling card.

"He set up my career," says Colin. "He has paid for a lot of these new buildings that are going up. He is the one who has been dragging in owners and dragging in jockeys. He has been everything and done everything for all of us.

"His first two runs shocked me to the core. When he won the Champion Bumper the back of my neck went stiff. Just talking about it now gives me goosebumps. That's my fondest memory of Cue Card."

It was a performance that made the young horse extremely valuable, as Jean Bishop well remembers.

"We had dinner with Colin and his wife Pauline not long after the Champion Bumper," she says.

"Colin was saying we were getting good offers and could get an awful lot of money if we sold him. After a while I started to get a bit cross. It seemed everyone was trying to talk us into selling.

"I said to Colin: 'Don't you want to train him?' To this day Colin still thinks I said: 'Can't you train him?' I think he thought that as this was a horse of a standard he hadn't had before I was questioning whether Colin was the right man to train him. I still have to tell him now that I didn't say what he thinks I said!"

The Bishops continued to own him, one Tizzard continued to train him, another Tizzard continued to ride him. Together they won a Haldon Gold Cup, then an Ascot Chase, a Ryanair Chase and a Betfair Chase, the jewel in Haydock's crown that Cue Card would win twice more, but by then with Brennan doing the steering.

"Haydock named a bar after Cue Card, which I opened," says Jean. "I was talking to a lady that day who said she follows Cue Card everywhere. She told me he means so much to her. She said she had suffered a lot of unhappiness in her life but that Cue Card had helped her deal with it."

Cue Card helped his fans (some of them fanatics), he helped his connections and he helped his sport. The joy of jump racing is our heroes and heroines keep coming back. It is hard to think of many who have come back as often as Cue Card. He returned season after season, and often following a significant reverse. He was a racehorse who won but also a racehorse who lost. From 41 outings there were 16 wins but therefore 25 defeats as well. He was not unbeatable, he was not infallible, he was not perfect – and he was all the better for all those things.

We will never forget Cue Card, but when we think of him we will inevitably think of those two Cheltenham Gold Cup falls, both sustained at the third-last fence, the first coming when he still looked for all the world to be full of running. Reflecting on that now, Bourne offers a different perspective, and says: "As Dad wasn't there, I think it would have been harder to have won the Gold Cup than it was to lose the Gold Cup. I think it would have been too emotional for us."

The truth is, we will never know what would have happened. Yet there is far more about Cue Card that we do know than we do not. We know he spent longer at the top than almost any horse in the sport's history. We know that when he was at his glorious best he was exceptional, such as when locking away his second Betfair Chase without coming off the bridle. We know he possessed a marvellous will to win, an asset that helped him courageously overhaul Vautour and avenge his dramatic King George defeat of two years earlier. We also know he loved being a racehorse, even in his senior stage. You only had to see him galloping with glee and attacking Ascot's fences as a top-class racing pensioner to be sure of that.

"He's 12 and he was still very good at Ascot, but time is catching up," said Colin Tizzard on the day of retirement, adding: "He won't leave the farm. He's going to stay here. I'm going to ride him round a bit to keep him active. He can stay here as long as he lives."

All being well, Cue Card will have many years being ridden by Colin around Venn Farm, where you can be sure members of the Bishop family will be regular visitors, there to see a horse they love and a horse Bob Bishop loved to talk about, right up until his passing.

"The consultant who was looking after Dad at the end told us later he had been telling her all about Cue Card," says Bourne. "She knew all about what had happened at Kempton. His last words would have been talking to her about Cue Card winning the King George."

For a true four-legged favourite of the people, the days of winning and running are now in the past. A chapter has closed. For the Bishops that has added meaning.

"I think we've felt that for all the time Cue Card has been racing, Dad has still been with us," says Bourne.

"It's only now Cue Card has stopped racing that we will properly start to grieve. Because Dad thought so much of Cue Card it has been as though we have still been with him and whenever Cue Card has been racing it has felt like Dad has still been with us. He carried on through Cue Card."

He still can. The memories made by Cue Card, a quite wonderful racehorse, are indelible.

We won't forget him.

Cue Card's owner Jean Bishop is joined by Colin Tizzard and son Joe as she signs a giant tribute card to the popular chaser at Sandown in April 2018

2014-15   2015-16   2016-17   2017-18

MAR | APR | NOV | DEC | JAN | FEB | MAR | APR | NOV | DEC | JAN | FEB | MAR | APR | NOV | DEC | JAN | FEB | MAR | APR | NOV | DEC | JAN | FEB | MAR | APR

RESULTS

(AT CLOSE OF 2017–18 SEASON)

CUE CARD (GB)
30 April 2006 bay gelding
King's Theatre (IRE) – Wicked Crack (IRE) (King's Ride (IRE))

TRAINER Colin Tizzard
OWNERS Bob and Jean Bishop
BREEDER Rowland Crellin

JUMPS PLACINGS 11/11242/1U212/15112/312/4452/4111F1/43121F2-F22P

LIFETIME RECORD	RUNS	WINS	2NDS	3RDS	WINNINGS	EARNINGS	OR	BEST TS	BEST RPR
Chase	34	12	9	2	£977,414	£1,343,822	166	161	180
Hurdle	5	2	2	0	£18,806	£67,996	151	148	152
NHF	2	2	0	0	£35,637	£35,637	—	119	138
Rules Races	41	16	11	2	£1,031,857	£1,447,454	—	—	—

DATE	RACE CONDITIONS	WGT	RACE OUTCOME	JOCKEY	OR	TS	RPR
15Mar18	Chl 2m5fSft C1ChG1 200K	11-10	PU/6 (Balko Des Flos 11-10) 9/2	P Brennan	166	—	0
17Feb18	Asc 2m5fSft C1ChG1 86K	11-7	2/7 (2¾L Waiting Patiently 11-7) 9/1	P Brennan	166	154	170
25Nov17	Hay 3m1½fHy C1ChG1 113K	11-7	2/6 (57L Bristol De Mai 11-7) 2/1	H Cobden	168	95	125
04Nov17	Wet 3mSft C1ChG2 57K	11-6	F/8 (Bristol De Mai 11-6) 5/2	P Brennan	168	—	0
06Apr17	Ain 3m1fGd C1ChG1 84K	11-7	2/7 (nk Tea For Two 11-7) 2/1F	P Brennan	170	134	168
17Mar17	Chl 3m2½fGd C1ChG1 327K	11-10	F/13 (Sizing John 11-10) 9/2	P Brennan	170	—	0
18Feb17	Asc 2m5fSft C1ChG1 85K	11-7	1/6 (15L Shantou Flyer 11-7) 4/9F	P Brennan	170	147	173
26Dec16	Kem 3mGd C1ChG1 119K	11-10	2/5 (3¾L Thistlecrack) 11-10 5/4	P Brennan	176	129	162
19Nov16	Hay 3mHy C1ChG1 120K	11-7	1/6 (15L Coneygree 11-7) 15/8F	P Brennan	176	156	176
29Oct16	Wet 3mGd C1ChG2 57K	11-10	3/7 (3¾L Irish Cavalier 11-6) 8/11F	P Brennan	176	116	165
27Apr16	Pun 3m1fGd/Y ChG1 88K	11-10	4/6 (6¾L Carlingford Lough 11-10) 4/6F	P Brennan	176	141	163
07Apr16	Ain 3m1fGS C1ChG1 85K	11-7	1/9 (9L Don Poli 11-7) 6/5F	P Brennan	176	112	176
18Mar16	Chl 3m2½fGd C1ChG1 327K	1-10	F/9 (Don Cossack 11-10) 5/2	P Brennan	176	—	180
26Dec15	Kem 3mGS C1ChG1 114K	11-10	1/9 (hd Vautour 11-10) 9/2	P Brennan	172	151	180
21Nov15	Hay 3mSft C1ChG1 113K	11-7	1/5 (7L Silviniaco Conti 11-7) 7/4	P Brennan	167	161	178
31Oct15	Wet 3mSft C1ChG2 57K	11-0	1/7 (3¾L Dynaste 11-0) 11/4F	P Brennan	160	120	167
29Apr15	Pun 3m1fGd/Y ChG1 95K	11-10	4/8 (15½L Don Cossack 11-10) 12/1	A Coleman	160	149	165
10Apr15	Ain 2m4fGd C1ChG1 113K	11-10	2/10 (26L Don Cossack 11-10) 6/1	D Jacob	163	129	158

DATE	RACE CONDITIONS	WGT	RACE OUTCOME	JOCKEY	OR	TS	RPR
26Dec14	Kem 3mGS C1ChG1 114K	11-10	5/10 (13L Silviniaco Conti 11-10) 11/2	D Jacob	171	134	164
22Nov14	Hay 3mSft C1ChG1 113K	11-7	4/9 (12L Silviniaco Conti 11-7) 3/1F	D Jacob	172	—	164
04Nov14	Exe 2m1½fGS C1HcChG2 36K	11-10	4/7 (15½L God's Own 10-7) 13/8F	D Jacob	172	129	165
26Dec13	Kem 3mSft C1ChG1 114K	11-10	2/9 (3½L Silviniaco Conti 11-10) 100/30J	J Tizzard	174	144	173
23Nov13	Hay 3mSft C1ChG1 113K	11-7	1/8 (4½L Dynaste 11-7) 9/1	J Tizzard	172	—	175
05Nov13	Exe 2m1½fGS C1HcChG2 36K	11-10	3/6 (6¼L Somersby 10-7) 11/10F	J Tizzard	172	113	172
05Apr13	Ain 2m4fGd C1ChG1 113K	11-10	2/6 (4½L Sprinter Sacre 11-10) 7/1	J Tizzard	170	115	178
14Mar13	Chl 2m5fGS C1ChG1 157K	11-10	1/8 (9L First Lieutenant 11-10) 7/2	J Tizzard	165	151	176
16Feb13	Asc 2m5fSft C1ChG1 84K	11-7	1/6 (6L Captain Chris 11-7) 15/8F	J Tizzard	165	155	170
26Dec12	Kem 3mHy C1ChG1 114K	11-10	5/9 (20L Long Run 11-10) 5/1	J Tizzard	165	81	153
06Nov12	Exe 2m1½fGS C1HcChG2 36K	11-7	1/5 (26L Edgardo Sol 11-7) 5/6F	J Tizzard	157	139	170
13Mar12	Chl 2mGd C1ChG1 74K	11-7	2/6 (7L Sprinter Sacre 11-7) 13/2	J Tizzard	155	156	167
31Dec11	Nby 2m2½fSft C3NvCh 7K	11-7	1/4 (4L For Non Stop 11-0) 5/2	J Tizzard	—	138	164
25Nov11	Nby 2m4fGd C1NvChG2 14K	11-8	2/4 (shd Bobs Worth 11-1) 2/1	J Tizzard	—	107	158
11Nov11	Chl 2m4½fGd C2NvCh 11K	11-7	UR/7 (Grands Crus 11-2) 7/4	J Tizzard	—	—	—
08Oct11	Chp 2m3½fGd C3NvCh 7K	11-4	1/4 (3½L Micheal Flips 11-4) 10/11F	J Tizzard	—	100	146
09Apr11	Ain 2m4fGd C1NvHG2 31K	11-4	2/9 (13L Spirit Son 11-4) 5/2F	J Tizzard	154	92	148
15Mar11	Chl 2m½fGd C1NvHG1 57K	11-7	4/15 (6½L Al Ferof 11-7) 7/4F	J Tizzard	159	148	150
11Dec10	Chl 2m1f GS C1HG2 86K	11-4	2/9 (4½L Menorah 11-4) 15/8	J Tizzard	160	135	152
12Nov10	Chl 2m½fGd C1NvHG2 14K	11-7	1/7 (8L Dunraven Storm 11-7) 8/13F	J Tizzard	—	146	152
24Oct10	Ain 2m4fGS C3NvH 5K	10-12	1/8 (13L Dear Sam 10-12) 1/2F	J Tizzard	—	78	144
17Mar10	Chl 2m½f Gd C1NHFG1 34K	10-12	1/24 (8L Al Ferof 11-5) 40/1	J Tizzard	121	119	138
25Jan10	Fon 1m5½fSft C6NHF 1K	10-7	1/13 (6L Caught By Witness 11-4) 6/1	J Tizzard	—	—	11

2014–15 | 2015–16 | 2016–17 | 2017–18

MAR | APR | NOV | DEC | JAN | FEB | MAR | APR | NOV | DEC | JAN | FEB | MAR | APR | NOV | DEC | JAN | FEB | MAR | APR | NOV | DEC | JAN | FEB | MAR | APR

CUE CARD b g 30-04-2006

King's Theatre b 1991	Sadler's Wells	Northern Dancer	Neartic → Nearco / Lady Angela
			Natalma → Native Dancer / Almahmoud
		Fairy Bridge	Bold Reason → Hail To Reason / Lalun
			Special → Forli / Thong
	Regal Beauty	Princely Native	Raise A Native → Native Dancer / Raise You
			Charlo → Francis S / Neutron
		Dennis Belle	Crafty Admiral → Fighting Fox / Admiral's Lady
			Evasion → Spy Song / Alnaire
Wicked Crack b 1993	King's Ride	Rarity	Hethersett → Hugh Lupus / Bride Elect
			Who Can Tell → Worden / Javotte
		Ride	Sovereign Path → Grey Sovereign / Mountain Path
			Turf → Ballymoss / Wood Fire
	Mighty Crack	Deep Run	Pampered King → Prince Chevalier / Netherton Maid
			Trial By Fire → Court Martial / Mitrailleuse
		Treize	Thirteen Of Diamonds → Mustang / Florrie
			Clear Bay → Baman / Clearhaven

Bred by Rowland Crellin